The Demographic Transition and Women's Life-course in Colombia

A demographic transition has, in any society, a direct effect on age distribution in its population. Some developing countries, like most of the industrialized countries, are experiencing the aging of their population structures due to a rapid decline in fertility rates. Such change has important implications at both the micro and macro levels of society. At the micro level, it implies different types of family composition and different processes of family formation. At the macro level, it means, among other things, different types of social demands on the state and pressures on the job market.

The Household, Gender, and Age Project of the United Nations University Programme on Human and Social Development conducted two case-studies – using life-course cohort analysis – in urban and rural areas in Colombia from 1983 to 1987 in order to understand the impact of its demographic transition in the last three decades on the lives of women and their families in different socio-economic strata in different geographical areas. This volume combines and compares the results of both studies and provides analyses of the complex interrelationships among women's education, labour participation, and family formation; socio-economic determinants in women's reproductive behaviour; women's perceptions of their life events; and the use of time and division of labour by gender and age within the household. It also includes discussion of future policy implications.

The Demographic Transition and Women's Life-course in Colombia

Carmen Elisa Florez

In collaboration with
Elssy Bonilla and Rafael Echeverri

UNITED NATIONS UNIVERSITY PRESS

The views expressed in this publication are those of the authors and do not necessarily reflect the views of the United Nations University.

United Nations University Press
The United Nations University, Toho Seimei Building, 15-1 Shibuya 2-chome, Shibuya-ku, Tokyo 150, Japan
Tel.: (03) 499-2811   Telex: J25442   Cable: UNATUNIV TOKYO

Typeset by Asco Trade Typesetting Limited, Hong Kong
Printed by Permanent Typesetting and Printing Co. Ltd., Hong Kong
Cover design by Tsuneo Taniuchi

HGA-1/UNUP-719
ISBN 92-808-0719-6
United Nations Sales No. E.90.III.A.1
03000 P

To my family

CONTENTS

Preface   ix

Introduction   xi

1. The Demographic Transition in Colombia   1

2. Methods and Data   5

3. General Characteristics   21

4. Women's Reproductive and Productive Behaviours over the Life-course   50

5. Women's Perceptions of Their Lives   100

6. Conclusions and Implications   124

   Appendix. Proportional Hazards Models Simplification   129

   Notes   141

   References   145

PREFACE

This book compiles and summarizes two studies, "The Impact of the Demographic Transition on Households in Bogotá" and "The Meaning of the Demographic Transition on Households of a Colombian Rural Setting," undertaken at the Center of Studies in Economic Development (CEDE) between 1984 and 1987. As such, it is the joint effort of many persons. As director of both studies, it is my privilege to thank Elssy Bonilla and Rafael Echeverri, who collaborated on parts of this volume, as well as others who participated in the research: Leonardo Garcia, Martha Rodriguez, and Diana Medrano. I especially want to thank Bernardo Guerrero, who worked with me on the design and implementation of the Bogotá urban longitudinal survey, and Argemiro Morales, who processed the raw life-history data with great skill.

I wish to express my appreciation and gratitude to Nohra Rey de Marulanda, researcher and director of CEDE in 1983, who conceived the original Bogotá urban study. I am also very grateful to Eleonora Masini, General Co-ordinator of the Household, Gender, and Age (HGA) Programme of the United Nations University (UNU), for her suggestions, comments, and encouragement. I wish also to thank HGA-UNU executive officer Kumiko Ishikawa, as well as HGA-UNU's consultant group, namely David Kertzer, Nancy Karweit, and Dennis Hogan, from whom we received support on different stages of the project. We are especially indebted to Nancy Karweit, who made available her Data Base Management Programme for Life History Data (CASA), enormously facilitating the retrieval of the data for the analysis.

The help of two groups of persons was critical to the urban and rural studies: the team of interviewers and the women who kindly responded to the surveys. Without them it would have been impossible to carry out these studies. I am also grateful to Leonel Castillo, who designed the sample for the urban longitudinal survey, and to Rafael Echeverri, one of the collaborators in this volume, who designed the rural sample and was responsible for both the urban and rural field-work.

I am profoundly grateful to the Household, Gender, and Age Programme of the United Nations University, to the Women's Status and Fertility Program of the Rockefeller Foundation for their financial support of the urban and rural projects, and to the National Administrative Department of Statistics in Colombia (DANE) for allowing us to use their computer facilities in processing the Bogotá urban survey. I appreciate the institutional support provided by the Demography Training Program of the University of Chicago, which awarded me a one-year Hewlett Foundation fellowship to revise and publish the urban and rural reports.

I especially want to thank Dennis Hogan, who, from the Population Issues Research Center of Pennsylvania State University, encouraged and supported me with his detailed feedback and suggestions during the revision and completion of this volume. I would also like to thank Douglas Massey, Marta Tienda, Nancy Denton, Robert Willis, Joseph Hotz, and John Craig for their support at the University of Chicago and for their extremely valuable comments on the earlier versions of this volume.

Lastly, a special thank you to Yolanda Butts for her patience in editing the English version of the manuscript.

Carmen Elisa Florez
Chicago, June 1988

INTRODUCTION

The Household, Gender, and Age (HGA) Programme of the United Nations University (UNU) promotes research on the effects at micro and macro levels of important and significant changes in developing societies. As part of that programme, the studies in this volume take the demographic transition in Colombia as the macro-level change and attempt to analyse its micro-level effects, its dynamic process, and its implications. One objective of the HGA-UNU programme is to encourage the use of life-course and time-allocation approaches in research about developing countries. These perspectives are well represented in this Colombian study through complete retrospective life-histories and reconstruction of time use during a normal week.

The study was restricted to the Andean region (Bogotá and the rural areas of Cundinamarca and Boyacá states), in view of the existence in Colombia of clearly distinguishable geographic and cultural regions with well-defined demographic and socio-economic characteristics. Conducting a national study of this kind, representing the different geographic regions, would have been of a magnitude almost impossible to handle. Given the sharp social and economic differentials existing in the country, the study is representative of the three broad socio-economic strata, lower, middle, and upper.

The analysis of the meaning of the demographic transition at the micro level is achieved by a comparison of the life-course of two cohorts of women representing the behaviour before and after the sharp and rapid decline in fertility experienced by Colombia at the beginning of the 1960s. Our study focused on women who were 25–29 (25–31) and on those who were 45–49 (40–49) years old in 1984 (1986) when the urban (rural) field-work was done. Hence, the study focuses on the *changes* in the demographic transitions characterizing the family formation process and its socio-economic determinants. A comparison of women's use of time and perceptions on aspects of productive and reproductive behaviours enriches and supports the longitudinal results.

Since we use both quantitative and qualitative methods, the research team represented a mix of disciplines appropriate to the study: economics and de-mography, sociology, and public administration. One investigator had consider-able experience in field-work.

This volume is organized in six chapters. The first documents the demographic transition process and the socio-economic changes experienced in Colombia dur-ing the last decades, and presents the main objectives of the study. Chapter 2 describes the research orientation, the methods of analysis for the life-course study, and the sample design and research instruments used in the urban and rural field-work, and discusses the quality of the collected data. The socio-economic characteristics of the geographic settings and the current socio-demographic char-acteristics of the women interviewed are analysed in chapter 3. Using the re-trospective life-histories, a comparative analysis is made in chapter 4 of the transi-tion processes women followed in forming their families and the socio-economic determinants of the likehood of those demographic events. The complex rela-tionship between women's work and the family formation process is also consi-dered in chapter 4 through an examination of female participation in productive activities as both influencing and being influenced by female reproductive be-haviour. Chapter 5 focuses on the analysis of women's perceptions of their family formation process, as well as on their use of time and the division of labour by gender and age within the household. The major conclusions of the study and their implications for policy in Colombia and for future research are discussed in chapter 6.

1

THE DEMOGRAPHIC TRANSITION
IN COLOMBIA

General Trends

Population trends in Colombia indicate that during the last five decades the country has been experiencing a demographic transition, a change from high to low birth and death rates. This process began toward the end of the 1930s when mortality conditions began to improve. Life expectancy[1] increased from 44 years in 1938 to 61 years in 1978, whereas the crude mortality rate decreased from 30.5 to 9 per thousand, and the infant mortality rate from 200.2 to 61 per thousand during the same 50-year period. By the beginning of the 1960s, fertility had started to decline, the total fertility rate[2] decreasing from 7.04 in 1960–1964 to 4.6 in 1972–1973, and to 3.6 in 1980, a reduction of almost 50 per cent in less than 20 years. The crude birth rate decreased from 45.2 at the end of the 1950s to 28.9 per thousand in 1980. The sharp decline in fertility during this period, especially before 1973 when the most important reductions occurred, has led many authors to characterize the experience of Colombia a "demographic transition without precedent" (Potter, Ordonez, and Meashman, 1976; Mauldin and Berelson, 1978). Figure 1 clearly shows the trends in mortality and fertility rates.

Although the fertility decline began first in the urban areas, and the country areas continue to lag behind, the rural decrease has been equally dramatic. Rural fertility levels in 1980 were as high as those in urban areas in 1968: a total rate of 5.1, but with a fertility pattern clearly affected by birth control. Rural reproductive behaviour has changed, but with a lag of almost 12 years in comparison to urban reproductive behaviour. According to the 1985 census, the total fertility rate was 3.2 for the nation, 2.7 for urban areas and 4.6 for rural areas (Florez, Echeverri, and Mendez, 1987).

During the same decades in which the country has experienced the demographic transition, important structural changes related to the development process have taken place. Without examining in detail the principal aspects of the socio-economic changes, we can mention the most important ones affecting population structure.

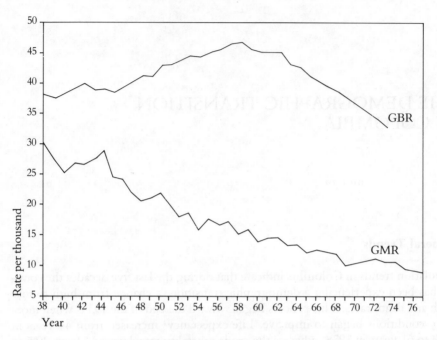

Fig. 1. The demographic transition in Colombia.

First, around 1950 the government began countrywide health campaigns geared toward the prevention of illness. Second, since 1956 there has been a remarkable increase in public expenditure on education, leading to a decrease in illiteracy from 47.7 per cent in 1938 to 20.6 per cent in 1973, and an increase in elementary-school attendance from 56.2 per cent in 1951 to 89.1 per cent in 1973. Third, the increase in public expenditure on education and health during the last 50 years has been nevertheless uneven, favouring urban over rural areas. This circumstance, together with the adoption of policies for the mechanization of agriculture in the 1950s and the stimulation of industry and construction in the 1960s and 1970s, created the conditions for an unprecedented migratory process during the 1960s. Rural–urban migration increased the degree of urbanization from 30.7 per cent in 1937 to 62 per cent in 1973; that is, the percentage of population residing in urban areas doubled in a 35-year period. Fourth, at the end of the 1960s the private sector began providing family planning services. These activities are permitted and tacitly supported by the government, thus accelerating the fertility decrease initiated at the beginning of the decade.

All these changes point to an understanding of how the modernization process and government policies in health and education combined to shape the demographic transition in Colombia. This process is expected to continue until at least the end of this century, although not with the intensity experienced during the 1960–1978 period. Our analysis suggests that, even after a stabilization phase has been achieved, large differences will persist between urban and rural areas, and between socio-economic sectors.

Objectives of the Study

A demographic transition has, in any population, a direct effect on age distribution, caused mostly by the strong decrease in fertility. Colombia's population structure is becoming older, and the relative proportion of infants is diminishing while the adult and elderly proportion is increasing. This change has important implications at both the micro and macro levels. At the micro level, for example, it implies different types of family composition and different processes of family formation. At the macro level, for the economy as a whole, this means, among other things, different types of social demands on the state and of pressures on the job market. Without a doubt, the demographic transition in Colombia has had an enormous impact on diverse spheres, many of which have not yet been analysed.

The speed with which demographic changes have occurred permits one to examine simultaneously households in which women were at reproductive ages when the total fertility rate reached its maximum level, and households where women were at reproductive ages after the fertility decline. Thus, the principal objective of our study has been to analyse the impact of Colombia's demographic transition at the micro (household) level through a comparison of the life-course of two groups of women: those who were at the peak of their fertility in the period 1960–1964 when fertility was at the maximum level (the 25–29 age-group at that time), and those who were at the peak of their fertility in 1980 (the most recent time at which information on fertility was available), and who were in the 20–24 age-group at that time. The comparison is made by examining changes between the two cohorts[3] in the different stages of the process of family formation and expansion, and by documenting the effects of women's status on the different demographic transitions characterizing the family formation process.

With the aim of complementing the quantitative longitudinal results, we examine family organization, and women's expectations and perceptions that are related to and determine the family formation process. Because of the large differences in income existing in the country, we stratify the sample into three socio-economic strata both in the urban and rural areas.

Given the magnitude of the study and the well-known differences in the urban and rural demographic transition process, two studies were conducted: one for an urban area, Bogotá, the capital of Colombia, and one for a rural area in the same geographical region (the Central Andean region). The necessary information for these studies was collected through a retrospective longitudinal survey (life-histories on residence, education, occupation, nuptiality, fertility, family planning, and co-residence), and case-studies on time allocation and perceptions and attitudes toward variables that determine women's productive and reproductive behaviour.

Study Design

The study of family formation as a dynamic process over life has not been approached in Colombia. In spite of the well-known decline in fertility experienced by the country during the last decades, all analyses have focused on cumulated and cross-section measures and interrelationships. Our approach, the life-course portrayed through retrospective data, provides interpretive richness and a better understanding of the changes and causes of the transition processes characterizing family formation. The methodology we use is not just a statistical method, but a general approach and research strategy beginning with data collection and continuing through data analysis.

Retrospective information is obtained from cohorts of women separated by an average of 20 years. In this way, the demographic events recorded reflect a range of historical and contextual experiences. The major problem with this type of design (that the experience of the most recent cohort examined is substantially incomplete right censoring) is dealt with by using life-table methods which do not assume that all those who will experience an event have already done so by the time of the data collection. Ethnomethodological and time-allocation in-depth studies complement the life-course analysis. This combination of quantitative with qualitative methods further enriches the analyses, and broadens the substantive interpretation we are able to give them.

Women are the primary unit of analysis for this study. The household, defined as a co-residential unit whose members share at least one of the three daily meals, is approached through the woman. A woman's behaviour and her perceptions with respect to the household and relevant variables are the core of the analysis.

To organize the analysis of urban and rural projects, we divided each into two parts: a longitudinal study and a qualitative and time-allocation study. In the longitudinal study we collected, for women from each cohort, two sets of information, one on the woman and her household's characteristics at the time of the interview, and another on her life-history of residence (migration), education, housework activities, occupation, nuptiality, fertility, family planning, and co-residence. The life-history information provides the basis for a multivariate analysis of women's reproductive and productive behaviour over time. In the qualitative and time-allocation study, we collect information on women's perceptions and roles, as well as on the division of labour within the household. This part of the study is done with a subsample of women from the longitudinal study because the in-depth interview needed for the case-studies was too time-consuming.

2

METHODS AND DATA

Research Orientation: The Life-course Approach

Most discussions of the demographic transition relate the decrease in fertility and mortality to changes in socio-economic and cultural variables associated with the modernization process (Coale, 1973; Freedman, 1979; Ryder, 1965; Caldwell, 1982). As such, it provides the general framework for this study. Within this broad framework, our main orientation is given by the perspective of life-history on human development (Elder, 1975, 1978, 1981; Featherman, 1983). This approach makes it possible to have a long-term historical perspective which produces a more dynamic analysis of demographic changes than the one used in conventional demographic studies.

Within the perspective of life-history we can see women's behaviour as conduct that develops continually throughout their lives as they grow and age in their social environment. This environment is characterized by the experiences and opportunities associated with the community, economic status, status within the family, and the normative and biological restrictions on sexual and age behaviour (Riley, 1973). The characteristics or status of women (education, marriage, participation in the labour force, occupational status, and income) define the context of their life-history in which demographic transitions occur. More specifically, this life-course perspective enables us to look at the influence of a woman's life-history (her status at each specific point in time) on the occurrence of the demographic events related to her family formation process (marriage, bearing of the first child, and so on). Thus, rather than analysing a cumulative process, like children ever born, as is commonly done, we are able to analyse the likelihood of occurrence of single events (transitions) affecting reproduction (marriage, fertility), as well as factors affecting their occurrence (transitions) over the life-span. It is possible here to examine the determinants of transitions between statuses here because of the retrospective longitudinal data we have obtained. Without such data we cannot study the factors affecting transitions.

The longitudinal dimension in the retrospective data describes sequences of events occurring over time. However, the spans of time covered by them do not include the complete life-histories of the women in our study. These vary in length from 25 to 49 years, depending on the cohort to which the women belong. While each life-history reflects the events that occurred from birth up to the moment of the survey, the lives of our women continue, of course, after the interview. Some women in the survey had experienced their first marriage, or had borne their first or second child or completed other demographic transitions by the date of the survey. Other women had not yet completed one or more of the transitions by the survey date, but might complete them later. For example, a childless woman at the time of the survey may have given birth to a child after the survey date. The experiences of women who have not yet completed a transition, but might complete one at a later age, are right censored by the date of the survey. This problem is especially acute among women in the younger cohort, whose experiences are censored by the survey date at a relatively early age (25–31 years). Fortunately, methods are available to surmount this problem. Proportional hazards life-table models, described below, provide a way of overcoming the censoring bias in the analysis of longitudinal data.

Ethnomethodology and time-allocation approaches are used to complement our dynamic longitudinal perspective. The postulates of the ethnomethodological school are used as much as possible in the study of women's perceptions. This approach is designed to comprehend the individuals and their social interaction, starting from the knowledge they have about themselves and about their actions. With it we can better understand women's perceptions on themes influencing their productive and reproductive behaviours, observed with the life-history data. With the time-allocation approach we can determine the division of work by sex and age inside the household. Women's attitudes and perceptions as well as the time distribution between household and productive activities may have changed as a consequence of the socio-economic modifications and the demographic transition.

The Study of Women's Life-course: Methods of Analysis

This section describes the methods that are used throughout the life-course analyses. Conventional demographic measurements such as nuptiality and fertility patterns and birth-control indexes (Coale and Trussell, 1974, 1978; Knodel, 1977) allow us to establish differentials between cohorts in purely demographic terms. Nuptiality and fertility models developed by Coale (Coale, 1971; Coale and Trussell, 1974) are used to identify the family formation process throughout its two principal phases: formation and expansion. Demographic studies have shown that marriage patterns (including legal and consensual unions) structure the course of fertility levels and have therefore made the proportion of unions by age a key element in the evaluation of the different configurations of fertility patterns. Marriage frequencies detect the probabilities of family forming and constitute the first object of analysis in the process of family formation itself. Age at first marriage is the classic measure for portraying a woman's experience in forming her family. The distribution of first unions by age can be obtained for any cohort by analysing the marriage (union) histories. From this point it is simple to determine the mean age at first union (marriage) for those women of the cohort who had experienced a union at the moment of the survey.

The experience in registered unions is more incomplete among younger cohorts. In spite of the truncation in marriage registrations for these cohorts, the mean age at first union can be estimated by adjusting Coale's standard curves of first marriage frequencies to the experienced marriages up to the date of the survey, assuming that future first marriages will follow the standard function. To adjust the first marriage model standard frequencies to the actual experience of the cohort,[1] three parameters must be estimated: G(w), the proportion of women ever married at age w, over which an insignificant proportion of women experience their first union; a_0, the earliest age in which a significant number of first marriages can be observed; and k, the factor that relates the pace at which marriages take place in a given cohort to the standard pace. A procedure of maximum likelihood is generally used. The two parameters a_0 and k determine the singulate mean age at first marriage (SMAM).[2]

The family begins to expand and to function as a reproductive unit with the birth of the first child. Fertility patterns and inter-birth intervals are then used to analyse the expansion phase of the family formation process. To smooth and estimate the observed age patterns of fertility, especially for the truncated experience of the younger cohort, Coale's model patterns of fertility were adjusted to the observed ones. Besides the parameters representing the first marriage pattern, one needs to estimate two parameters:[3] m, the degree to which birth control affects the marital fertility pattern in the studied population; and M, a scale factor which expresses the level of the actual marital fertility around age 20 with respect to the natural fertility. The model patterns have proved to be a good approximation of the actual experiences of different populations, even though it includes neither illegitimate births nor marriage dissolutions. However, when the proportion of illegitimate births is relatively high, age at first marriage is not a good indicator of the age at which cohabitation begins. In these cases the distribution by age at first birth is a good substitute for the pattern of the beginning of cohabitation.

When considering the fertility patterns that synthetically connect fertility to age, the fact that women of the same age can be at different stages of family formation is left aside. Fertility analysis is enriched by studying the transition process from one parity to another, taking into account not only the fertility intensity, seen in this case as the proportion of women that have a child of a certain order during a given time interval, but also the time distribution in the transition process from one parity to another. The technique we used is the elaboration of life tables applied to the protogenesic interval (interval between marriage and the birth of the first child) and to inter-birth intervals. The use of this procedure permits the elimination of the "censoring effect," that is, the distortions resulting from open intervals by the date of the interview.

The demographic methods mentioned do not permit a full exploitation of the available longitudinal data. To be more specific, they do not allow us to examine the determinants of transitions between statuses, to consider simultaneously the effect of various independent variables on the likelihood of occurrence of the demographic events, or to interrelate them at the time when the demographic events occur. However, statistical techniques especially designed for the analysis of life-history data (Tuma, Hannan, and Groeneveld, 1979; Menken, Trussell, Stempel, and Babakol, 1981; Trussell and Hammerslough, 1983) allow us to develop the multivariate analysis of the reproductive behaviour of women throughout their lives. We use, specifically, the proportional hazards life-table models first proposed by Cox (1972) and later developed by Breslow (1974), Holford (1976), and Kalbfleisch and Prentice (1980). These models allow us to manipulate censored observations (those that have not experienced the event at the time of the last observation or time of interview) and produce measurable estimates of the effects of two or more independent variables that operate in a multivariate framework. The analytical tool of the models is still the life table, but we can assume that the duration (time) of specific risk rates for individuals with different characteristics is proportional, with proportionality factors that are constant for each duration.[4] The models are centred on two related functions, the survival function S(t) and the risk function h(t). The survival function to an event gives the probability that an individual survives at least until time t (or equivalently until age a) without the event having occurred. The risk function defines the probability of the event occurring if it has not taken place before time t (or age a).

These models are formulated in terms of the effects of the covariates (independent variables) on the rate of risk that a given event will occur. If h (t;Z) represents the risk function in time t for an individual with a vector of covariates Z, the relation between the risk function and the covariates at each point in time can be represented by:[5]

$$h(t;Z) = h_0(t) \exp(B'Z)$$

where B' is an unknown regression coefficient vector and $h_0(t)$ is the unknown baseline risk function for individuals with a vector of covariates $Z = 0$ $(z_1 = z_2 = \ldots z_n = 0)$. The baseline risk function is totally arbitrary and need not be defined by a parametric model. Each one of the coefficients indicates the effect of the independent variable over the baseline risk function. A coefficient b_k equal to 0 [or $\exp(b_k) = 1$] indicates no effect. Positive values [or $\exp(b_k) > 1$] indicate that individuals with this characteristic probably will experience a given event (quantity) and will do so more rapidly as well (pace). The opposite occurs with negative coefficients [$\exp(b_k) < 1$]. Parameters are estimated by partial likelihood procedures with the statistical properties of unbiasedness and normality (Allison, 1984).

The proportional hazards model is extraordinarily general and non-restrictive. Although the model describes many situations, sometimes there are important factors which produce hazards functions that do not satisfy the proportionality assumption. For instances where the assumption is violated, Kalbfleisch and Prentice (1980) suggest an extension of the model called "stratification" allowing for non-proportionality. The idea is to group the data into "strata" according to the variable for which the assumption may be violated. The hazards function for an individual in the jth stratum (or level) is defined as:

$$h_j(t;Z) = h_{0j}(t) \exp(B'Z)$$

where $j = 1, 2, \ldots q$ represent the "strata," Z is the vector of convariates, and $h_{0j}(t)$ is the baseline hazard function for the jth strata at time t, which is allowed to be arbitrary and unrelated. Thus, under this extension of the model, the arbitrary hazard function $h_{0j}(t)$ is allowed to be different for each stratum, while the regression coefficients are the same across strata. The coefficient for the extended model can be estimated using partial likelihood procedures, as with the basic models. Statistics analogues of nonparametric rank tests but appropriate for censored data can be used to test whether proportionality holds across strata (Kalbfleisch and Prentice, 1980).

Since our main objective with this model is to examine the determinants of transitions between statuses, the covariates in the models refer to those independent variables that affect the likelihood of transitions characterizing the family formation process, that is, marrying, and bearing the first, the second, and the third child. Women's status indicators, as well as other socioeconomic and demographic (control) variables, are included as covariates. The expected relationships are explained in the following section.

Conceptual Framework: Women's Status, Nuptiality, and Fertility Interrelationships

This section provides the conceptual framework used to characterize how the relationship between women's status and socio-economic variables (covariates) influences the family formation process (nuptiality and fertility) over the lifespan.

Numerous empirical indicators of female status have been used in the socio-demographic literature (UN, 1984). Some of the most commonly used ones are measures of women's labour-force participation and educational attainment.

Both usually exert a positive statistical relationship on nuptiality and specifically on female age at marriage. Women's education may influence age at marriage through its effect on participation in extra-domestic employment before marriage (Standing, 1978). Pre-marital employment may increase a woman's age at first marriage because the impact that work has on women's own aspirations and attitudes fosters greater independence and autonomy.

The factor most consistently shown to determine women's status and to influence their fertility is education. Women's education may affect age at marriage, which in turn affects fertility. This is because education provides women with knowledge and resources that may increase their status and autonomy, which in turn affects fertility decisions. Better educated women often use contraception at high rates, which certainly reduces fertility. Education influences women's employability and wage levels, which in turn influence the opportunity cost of a female's time affecting fertility.

The relationship between women's labour-force participation and fertility can be analysed from complementary economic and sociological perspectives. The first perspective is based on micro-economic theories of household decision-making (Becker, 1960, 1965), and focuses primarily on the opportunity cost of children. This cost derives from the economic theory of time allocation in which the value (or cost) of time allocated to a particular activity is determined by the value of its best alternative use, approximated by the relevant market wage. According to this perspective, the higher the opportunity cost, the lower the fertility level (Willis, 1973). The opportunity cost of children may rise due to increases in female education, which in turn increases labour-market opportunities for women.

An alternative perspective, called the role-incompatibility hypothesis, focuses on the interaction between the roles of mother and working woman. Essentially, the more incompatible mother and worker roles are, the more negative the labour-force participation–fertility relationship. In traditional rural societies where agricultural work prevails, mother and worker roles can be combined without difficulty; hence there will be no relationship between fertility and work. In modern urban societies where economic and social life are structured in such a way that it is difficult to combine both child-rearing and employment, an inverse relationship will emerge. Where role incompatibility exists, it generally increases with higher education and rising opportunity costs. The role prevailing will depend on the opportunity cost of children. The two perspectives, then, are entirely consistent and complementary.

A variety of work-related factors must be considered in the analysis of employment and fertility interrelationships. The type and condition of work also influence the nature of the relationship. Women who work for a salary outside their homes will experience greater role incompatibility than women in other work conditions. Women employed in the modern sector have less flexible work schedules than services or home workers.

When examining the effects of women's status variables on nuptiality and fertility, it is necessary to control for other socio-economic variables which also may affect the strength of the relationship, such as origin and place of residence. A good deal of empirical work has shown that the employment and fertility relationship is negative in urban areas and either positive or non-existent in rural areas. This is largely explained by the fact that agricultural work in rural areas is less incompatible with childbearing (UN, 1985). Place of residence also affects individual decision-making through the presence (or not) in the community of contraceptive services, health facilities, schooling opportunities, and economic opportunities and costs (Cochrane, 1983). On the other hand, place of origin can affect educational opportunities and then determine educational achievements.

Empirical evidence also suggests the desirability of including the husband's characteristics and community variables in the study of fertility determinants. However, the life-course approach requires information on the husband's life-history, and collecting this information would have greatly increased the cost of the study. For that reason, and given the lesser importance of husband characteristics on fertility determination, we focus only on women's characteristics. Community variables throughout a woman's life are only captured by urban–rural characterization of the different places the women have lived.

The Data

Sample Design in Urban and Rural Areas

The area of study of the urban survey is restricted to Bogotá, the capital of Colombia. The sample universe of the urban (Bogotá) study[6] is composed of those women between the ages of 25 and 29, and 45 and 49, living in Bogotá in private houses between May and June 1984, excluding women residing in collective housing. These two cohorts represent the behaviour before and after the demographic transition.[7] The urban survey had a probabilistic, pre-stratified and two-stage sample of unequal conglomerates. The sample universe was stratified according to the housing inventory of the dwelling units in the city compiled by the National Department of Statistics (DANE) in 1980–1981 (Sise–DANE, 1982). Although this inventory classified the dwellings in six strata according to external observation of the buildings (type of construction, quality of the unit, availability of utilities, location, and other data related to housing), we reclassified them into only three strata: low, middle, and upper. In the first sample stage, clusters were selected, and in the second the dwelling units were selected according to the size of the already selected clusters.

The target urban sample of 1,500 women (750 in each cohort) led to visits to 6,756 dwellings in 360 clusters (120 in each stratum), from which it was possible to get information from 6,012 (a coverage of 93 per cent). In these selected dwell-

Table 1. Urban sample results

Characteristic	Stratum			
	Low	Middle	Upper	Total
Selected dwellings	2,399	2,144	2,213	6,756
Interviewed dwellings	2,269	1,920	1,823	6,012
Dwellings coverage rate (%)	94.6	89.6	82.2	89.0
Interviewed households	3,693	2,858	1,879	8,430
Households/dwelling	1.6	1.5	1.0	1.4
Household size	4.6	4.5	4.5	4.5
Selected women				
Younger cohort[a]	265	218	147	630
Older cohort[b]	181	230	212	623
Interviewed women				
Younger cohort	258	188	132	578
Older cohort	164	186	145	496
Women's coverage rate (%)				
Younger cohort	97.4	86.2	89.8	91.7
Older cohort	90.6	80.9	68.4	79.5

a. The 25–29-year-old cohort.
b. The 45–49-year-old cohort.

ings there were 8,430 households. Table 1 summarizes these urban sample results. The average number of households per dwelling unit for the city as a whole was about 1.5, which varied considerably by stratum, from 1.6 in the lower stratum to 1.0 in the upper stratum. On the other hand, the average size of the household was similar by stratum, about 4.5 persons per household.

The selected urban households included 630 women in the younger cohort and 623 women in the older cohort. Of these women, 91.7 per cent in the younger cohort and 79.5 per cent in the older cohort agreed to give an interview, giving a total of 578 and 496 completed interviews. This coverage rate is in the same range as other demographic surveys in Bogotá. The results, however, differ by stratum. As expected, the lowest coverage was obtained among the older cohort in the upper stratum, 68.4 per cent and the highest among the youngest cohort in the lower stratum, 97.4 per cent. The sample coverage by stratum was affected by two factors: the dwellings coverage rate (89 per cent average) and the women's coverage rate by cohort (an average of 91.7 and 79.5 per cent).

The rural study was conducted as a basis of comparison with the Bogotá urban study. For this reason, and in order to control for differentials resulting from different cultural patterns, the rural areas chosen had geographical and cultural patterns similar to Bogotá. The analysis of migration flows to Bogotá indicated

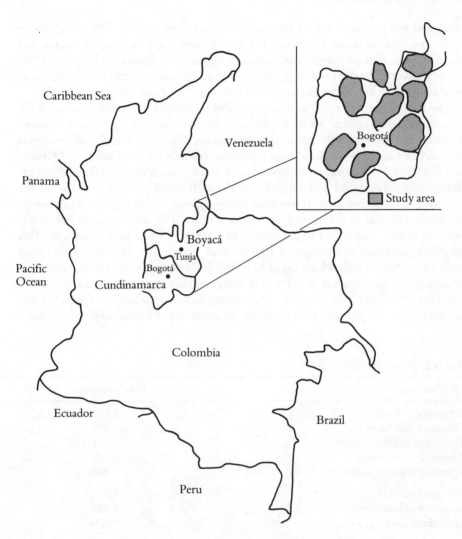

Fig. 2. Colombian rural longitudinal survey.

that Boyacá and Cundinamarca states account for almost 80 per cent of the total migrants. The area of study was first defined as the rural zones of Boyacá and Cundinamarca states, located in the higher areas of the Andean region.[8] However, the delimited rural area has relatively homogeneous characteristics of economic production and land tenancy relations, and its townships are very close to those covered by the Rural Integrated Development (DRI) government programme.[9] Given the existence of basic information about the DRI programme areas and the potential use of the results of this study by the DRI programme itself, the area of study was restricted to the rural areas of Cundinamarca and Boyacá townships (dispersed rural areas and head townships with less than 1,000 people) covered by the DRI programme. Figure 2 shows the rural areas chosen as well as the location of the city of Bogotá, where the urban survey was made.

The two cohorts of rural women representing the periods before and after the demographic transition were 40–49 and 25–31 years of age[10] in October–November 1986 when the field-work was done. The rural sample universe was then defined as the women in those two focus cohorts[11] living, between October and November 1986, in private households in the chosen rural areas. The sample design was two-staged and probabilistic,[12] with equal probabilities for all the elements of the population. It was thus self-weighing. In the first stage townships were selected, and in the second the dwelling units. The target sample size of 600 women in each cohort led to a selection of 3,600 dwellings in 360 clusters. This implicitly assumed an average of 10 dwellings per cluster. However, we found only an average of 9.8, which led us to visit 3,537 dwellings, of which 3,284 were occupied (7.1 per cent vacancy rate). It was possible to get information for 3,059 dwellings (93.0 per cent coverage), containing 3,369 households, of which 3,133 co-operated (93.0 per cent coverage). In the interviewed households, 570 women

Table 2. Rural sample results

Characteristic	N or percentage
Selected dwellings	3,537
Occupied dwellings	3,289
Dwellings vacancy rate (%)	7.1
Interviewed dwellings	3,059
Dwellings coverage rate (%)	93.0
Selected households	3,369
Interviewed households	3,133
Household coverage rate (%)	93.0
Selected women	
Younger cohort[a]	570
Older cohort[b]	638
Interviewed women	
Younger cohort	533
Older cohort	578
Women's coverage rate (%)	
Younger cohort	93.5
Older cohort	90.6

a. The 25–31-year-old cohort.
b. The 40–49-year-old cohort.

were selected for the younger cohort, and 638 for the older cohort. Of these women, 533 in the younger cohort and 578 in the older cohort agreed to be interviewed, producing a coverage of 93.5 and 90.6 per cent respectively. Table 2 summarizes the rural sample results. The total coverage of the rural survey was then affected by four factors: the dwelling vacancy rate (7.1 per cent); the dwelling coverage rate (93.0 per cent); the household coverage rate (93.0 per cent); and the coverage rate of individual women by cohort (93.5 and 90.6 per cent).

In order to control for and analyse women's reproductive and productive behaviours in the rural area according to socio-economic life conditions, we post-stratified the townships, the households, and the women *ex post facto*. Households were stratified by their dwelling-place conditions, not solely by their own characteristics. Three socio-economic strata were defined according to the conditions of the household (quality), tenancy relations, economic support source, isolation, community services access, and community organization.[13] The low stratum was the third of the households that had the poorest infrastructure and the most precarious production conditions. The middle stratum was the next third of the households and the upper strata the top one-third, classified by these aspects of well-being. These strata permitted us to define homogeneous population groups. Women were then classified in the socio-economic strata according to the households to which they belonged. Table 3 presents the distribution of selected and interviewed women in the rural area by cohort and socio-economic strata.

Given the characteristics of the qualitative, time-allocation in-depth urban and rural studies, it was impossible to include all the women to which the life-history questionnaire was applied in this part of the study. Therefore, it was necessary to select a group of 30 women in each urban and rural area, 15 from each cohort,

Table 3. Distribution of selected and interviewed women by cohort and stratum, rural area

	Stratum			
Characteristic	Low	Middle	Upper	Total
Selected women				
Younger cohort[a]	149	195	225	570
Older cohort[b]	200	225	214	638
Interviewed women				
Younger cohort	145	180	208	533
Older cohort	179	204	195	578
Women's coverage rate (%)				
Younger cohort	95.2	92.5	91.2	93.5
Older cohort	87.1	91.5	92.2	90.6

a. The 25–31-year-old cohort.
b. The 40–49-year-old cohort.

with the aim of developing an in-depth study to identify the possible changes between cohorts in women's conceptions of their lives. The criterion used in the selection of the women for this study was the goal of maximizing variation along several dimensions. The definition of the cases included an analysis of the variables nuptiality, fertility, work, socio-economic stratum, and age.

Since the objective of the in-depth part of the study was to complement the longitudinal study (not to obtain a statistical representation but rather to portray typical cases), the selection was carried out by taking the life-history interviews as the sample framework to which a probabilistic selection method was applied. Among the 30 women in the urban area sample, 20 per cent were from the upper stratum, 33 per cent from the middle and 47 per cent from the lower stratum. In the rural area, the 30 women interviewed had a distribution by stratum equal to the urban area.

Questionnaire Design

Urban and rural studies basically made use of the same questionnaire to obtain data on the women's life-history. The questionnaire is standard; it uses a flow design and response alternative, and is precoded according to certain predictable criteria defining certain alternative answers. It was designed with a structured format to gather two sets of information, one on the woman and her household characteristics at the moment of the interview and another on her life-history. The first part contains information on the members of the households of the selected woman, such as kinship, age, sex, marital status, wage-earning activity, and housework activities. It also contains characteristics of the woman's parents (education and work activity when the woman was 15 years old) and her characteristics at the moment of the interview as control variables for her life-history. Moreover, the rural study had prospective variables related to women's opinions and expectations with respect to their children's education and women's economic support in old age, as well as women's work outside the home.

The second part of the questionnaire has information about the sequences of events in a woman's life on the following variables: residence, education, paid work, non-paid work (housework as well as, in rural areas, activities that are related to agricultural production for household consumption and/or non-agricultural business), nuptiality (legal and consensual unions), fertility, other pregnancies, family planning and co-residence. This part was structured as a matrix in which rows correspond to the woman's age or the dates (calendar years) and the columns, grouped by headings or subjects, correspond to the measured variables.

The rural study made use of two additional instruments for gathering information at the cluster and household levels. The cluster questionnaire gathered information necessary for the post-stratification units such as altitude, isolation characteristics – distances to urban and trading areas for articles produced in the clusters, existence of main roads, schools and health centres, accessibility to the community, existence of community services such as permanent health promoters, drugstores, power and water supply services – and community organized groups represented by public action boards, committees, and co-operatives. The household questionnaire gathered information on characteristics of both the dwelling unit and the household itself. The dwelling characteristics referred to the unit typology, availability of basic water service, number of bedrooms, and number of households living in the same dwelling unit. This information makes it possible to estimate the quality of life of the population. Household characteristics referred to land ownership, cooking utensils, and basic source of subsistence, as well as characteristics of the members of the household such as relation to the household head, sex, age, marital status, and economic activities, whether remunerated or not.

The urban and rural studies used basically the same questionnaires to gather information for the in-depth case studies, with the necessary adjustments to the conditions and experiences of the urban or rural women. Two different instruments were used to collect data. First, a highly detailed guideline was developed for the interviews, where the principal factor considered was detection of women's ideas, opinions, reflections and attitudes on matters such as marriage, family size, sexuality, maternity, abortion, family planning, cohabitation, migration, work, power relations within the family, and female participation in different social contexts.

Secondly, with the aim of gathering information related to the use and distribution of time, a subgroup of 10 women in each urban and rural study was selected. In order to investigate the division of labour inside the household, a chart time allocation was designed to map the different activities undertaken by the women in the domestic context, in the productive (paid or not) and child-caring spheres as well as during leisure time. It also included a section on the different activities undertaken by the husband, as perceived by the women. This instrument helped show the length of time devoted to each activity undertaken during the weekday as well as weekend days for both the woman and her husband. The following domestic activities were taken into account: cooking, washing, ironing, house cleaning, grocery shopping, getting water and fuel for cooking, taking care of domestic animals, carrying food to spouses or sons at their place of work, and taking the children to school. As for productive activities (remunerated or not), the principal and secondary occupations were established: the occupational position of every activity, the place, the frequency during the week, the length, and the contributions of other members of the family. For households with children under age 6, it was determined which members of the family were responsible for their care and which members were helping.

Video equipment was used in the rural area with a subsample of six women. The intent was to record images around specific activities such as the process of cooking, mealtimes, specific productive activities undertaken by the woman, and the manipulation of tools. The main objective of using the video camera was to strengthen the observational capacities of the researchers.

Data Quality

As with any other life-history study, this study is vulnerable to the selective effects of mortality. In any population cross-section, the surviving members of older birth cohorts are less fully representative of their cohorts at some earlier time than the survivors of younger cohorts (Featherman, 1980). Thus, cross-sectional life-history studies tend to underrepresent the earlier experiences of older cohorts as a function of differential mortality. However, when mortality declines, the major changes are usually observed below age 5 (or even 10) or at the older ages. Mortality changes in the middle age-groups are much less important. Thus, we would expect that the proportion surviving from age 15 to age 45 is similar in a current life table to a life table of 30 years ago. The representativeness of our younger and older cohorts is similar and the type of bias due to this type of selectivity may be very small.

Another selectivity problem with retrospective life-history data arises from emigration. However, the fact that the urban and rural studies are related precisely by the variable migration partly remedies this problem. We must remember that about 80 per cent of total migrants to Bogotá come from the states selected for the rural survey.

Retrospective reports are also subject to errors of recall. However, checks on internal consistency at the time of the interview enhance the reliability of the data. The cross-sectional part of the information at the time of the survey permits the control of the information gathered on the life-histories. Additionally, the design of the life-history matrix itself allows for internal consistency; specifically, the matrix was filled by variables (columns) and, as each history variable was filled in, it was checked against the other life domains for which information had already been provided. This design allowed us to check for the internal consistency of the data and facilitated accuracy in the recall of the ages or dates of occurrence of the different events.

Since additional validation of the quality of the data has been done for infant mortality analyses using the fertility life-history data (Florez and Hogan, 1988a) and for women's time-allocation analysis using the complete set of life-histories (Florez and Hogan, 1988b), we may conclude that the data collected in both the urban and rural longitudinal surveys is of sufficient quality to conduct this life-course study.

The analysis of women's attitudes and perceptions refers to the moment of the interview. In order to check for differences of opinion in different situations, different dimensions of the aspects under study were considered.[14] Emphasis was given to women's opinions referring to their own experiences, their mother's experiences, and their daughters' expected behaviour. The use of a video camera as a research instrument requires a previously accepted and empathic relationship between the research population and the researcher. This allows the filming of the different situations as normally experienced by the studied person. Otherwise, the situation can become very artificial, impeding registration of the various processes as they normally occur. In spite of this limitation, the filmed material provided a better understanding of the factors which organize people's behaviour.

Summary

This study employs the life-course approach to gather retrospective life-history data to analyse the transition processes characterizing family formation and to conduct a causal analysis of those transition processes among women representing the behaviour before and after the demographic transition in Colombia. Given the sharp income differentials existing in the country, the study takes into account three socio-economic strata: low, middle and upper. Coale's nuptiality and fertility models are used to identify the family formation process. Since life-history data is right censored by the survey date, we used proportional hazards life-table models to overcome this censoring bias and produce measurable estimates of the effects of various independent variables that operate in a multivariate framework. Women's status indicators such as educational attainment and labour-force participation, as well as other socio-economic variables such as origin and place of residence, are considered as influencing the family formation transitions over the life-course. Data on the division of labour inside the household and on women's attitudes and perceptions of their lives on those socio-economic aspects influencing family formation are also gathered with the aim of complementing the life-course analyses. The analysis of this data is done using, as much as possible, the postulates of the ethnomethodological school, which attempts to understand individuals and their social interactions on the basis of the knowledge they have about themselves and about their actions.

An urban and a rural area of the central Andean region were sampled in order to produce a basis for comparative study: the urban centre of Bogotá, the capital of Colombia, and the rural areas of Boyacá and Cundinamarca townships (dispersed rural areas and townships with less than 1,000 people) covered by the Integrated Rural Development (DRI) programme. A probabilistic, pre-stratified, and two-stage sample of unequal clusters in the urban area led to interviews with 579 women in the younger cohort and 496 in the older cohort. A two-stage and probabilistic sample was used in the rural area, leading to interviews with 533 women in the younger cohort and 578 women in the older cohort. In order to control for socio-economic stratum in the rural area, a post-stratification of the townships, the households, and the women was generated. For the qualitative in-depth urban and rural studies, a subsample of 30 women was selected in each area, 15 from each cohort. Of those, 10 were selected in each area for an analysis of their time allocation and division of labour inside the household.

The questionnaire for women's life-history was designed in a structured format which included a cross-section part for control variables and a matrix to record the sequences of events. This design allowed the interviewers to check for internal consistency of the data and facilitated accuracy in the recall of the different events. The questionnaire for the in-depth case-studies on women's perceptions was designed in a semi-structured format to produce a flexible interview. A chart time allocation was designed to outline the different productive and reproductive activities performed by the woman and other members of her household. A video camera was used with a subsample of women in the rural area to gather more detailed information on their environments, life-styles, and their division of labour inside the household.

3

GENERAL CHARACTERISTICS

This chapter describes the characteristics of the urban and rural research sites, and the characteristics of the interviewed women at the time of the survey. The first section focuses on the socio-economic characteristics of Bogotá and the rural zones of the study. It examines the conditions of the sites themselves, as well as at the characteristics of their population. The description of the urban area uses available secondary information, whereas for the rural area we use the data collected at the community and household level. The second section of this chapter focuses on socio-economic and demographic characteristics of the respondents, and provides a global view of women's background and current conditions at the moment of the interview.

Geographic Settings

Bogotá

Bogotá is the capital city of Colombia. Like other Latin American countries, Colombia experienced urban growth at an accelerated rate in the post-Second World War era. However, this growth process has shown specific differences in Colombia, where the population has been concentrated in four major centres: Bogotá, Cali, Medellín and Barranquilla. This contrasts with the majority of the countries, which have concentrated most of their urban growth in a single metropolis. In all Latin America, Bogotá is the capital city with the lowest index of urban concentration in relation to the rest of the country.

Bogotá remains an economic and demographic centre as a result of urban development and of this system of cities. Parallel to the urbanization process, which

This chapter was written in collaboration with Rafael Echeverri.

Table 4. Population trends, Colombia and Bogotá, 1938–1985 (percentages)

Year	Urban/ Colombia	Bogotá/ Colombia	Growth rate		
			Total Colombia	Urban Colombia	Bogotá
1938	31.0	3.8	—	—	—
1951	39.0	5.7	2.2	3.9	5.2
1964	52.0	9.5	3.2	5.4	7.3
1973	59.0	12.5	2.5	3.7	5.6
1985	67.2	14.3	2.1	3.2	3.2

Source: National Administrative Department of Statistics (DANE), Colombian censuses.

increased the proportion of the national urban population from 31 per cent in 1938 to 59 per cent in 1973, was an increase in Bogotá's population concentration from 3.8 per cent in 1938 to 12.5 per cent in 1973. The large rural–urban migration flows during the 1960s led to Bogotá's high population growth-rate during the 1964–1973 intercensus period: 7.3 per cent, while the rate for the country as a whole was 3.2 and the total urban average rate was 3.4. It is clear from table 4, which presents trends in population growth for Bogotá as well as for the country, that in the 1970s the population growth-rates began to decline steadily. In the case of Bogotá this was a consequence of the stabilization of the migration flows to the city and of the decrease in fertility.

Distribution of the dwellings by socio-economic stratum indicates the existence of large income differentials in the city. For statistical purposes and socio-economic analysis, the National Administrative Department of Statistics, DANE, classified the city's dwellings in six socio-economic strata in 1980, according to their characteristics and accessibility to services (Sise–DANE, 1982). Table 5 presents that classification. While 2.5 per cent of the dwellings corres-

Table 5. Distribution of households in Bogotá, by socio-economic strata, 1980

Stratum	No. of households	%
Low-low	13,519	2.5
Low	111,680	20.6
Middle-low	247,656	45.7
Middle	110,902	20.5
Middle-high	43,609	8.1
High	14,339	2.6
Total	541,705	100.0

Source: National Administrative Department of Statistics (DANE), 1982.

Table 6. School attendance rates, by age-group and sex, Bogotá (percentages)

Age-group	Male	Female	Total
5–6	63.1	64.2	63.6
7–11	93.2	93.5	93.4
12–17	81.3	78.4	79.8
18–24	37.5	34.8	36.0
25–34	12.1	10.1	11.0
35–44	4.0	4.3	4.1
45–49	1.7	2.3	2.0
60+	1.6	1.5	1.6
Total	34.6	33.5	34.6

Source: 1985 Colombian Census.

pond to a very low socio-economic level (that is, housing without utilities), 20.5 per cent are low-level popular housing with some access to utilities, 74.4 per cent are middle-class housing with most utilities, and only 2.6 per cent are upper-level housing.

Bogotá, as capital of the country, has very good accessibility to educational and health services. This has important cultural and economic implications for its population. According to the 1985 Colombian population census, the literacy rate for the population older than 5 years of age was about 92.3 per cent, slightly higher for males (92.9 per cent) than for females (91.8 per cent). This testifies to the high degree of access to the educational system in the city. Educational levels in general are determined by attendance rates. Table 6 presents the attendance rates of the population over 5 years of age by sex and age-group. The general pattern of formal school attendance in Bogotá is similar for males and females. It indicates that there is an early entrance of the population to school, but that students start dropping out of the system by the end of high school. It is clear that the highest attendance rates, 93.4 per cent, occur among the 7–11 age-groups irrespective of sex. This rate implies an almost universal attendance at primary school. Similarly, a high attendance rate of 79.8 per cent is observed among the 12–17 age-group, which corresponds to secondary level. However, after age 18 the attendance rates decline for both males and females, implying either completion of secondary school, dropping out, or non-continuation to post-secondary school.

The educational profile in 1985 for the Bogotá population older than 5 years of age is presented in table 7. There are no major differences in the profiles by sex and the levels are relatively high when compared with the rest of Colombia. About 8.2 per cent of the population has no education, and about 75 per cent has finished primary school. Although almost two-thirds of those who finished

Table 7. Distribution of the population of five years and older, by educational level and sex, Bogotá (percentages)

Education	Male	Female	Total
None	7.8	8.7	8.2
Incomplete primary	16.5	16.2	16.6
Complete primary	22.4	22.7	22.4
Incomplete secondary	26.2	28.2	27.5
Complete secondary	10.9	11.7	11.2
Superior or more	13.6	9.8	11.7
No information	2.6	2.4	2.4
Total	100.0	100.0	100.0
N (thousands)	1,646	1,863	3,509

Source: 1985 Colombian Census.

elementary school go on to higher levels of education, more than half of them drop out before finishing secondary level and only about one-fourth get into superior or higher levels of education. These educational profiles suggest an incapacity of the educational system to retain its population at the secondary level and a low access to superior levels of education.

According to the 1985 population census, about 54 per cent of the Bogotá population aged 12 and over was participating in economically productive activities (employed plus unemployed). This rate of participation, however, is highly differentiated by sex. Whereas 70 per cent of the male population was engaged in productive activities, only 40.3 per cent of women were doing so. Although this female participation is lower than the rate for males, it is relatively high for a country like Colombia.

Rural Areas

CHARACTERISTICS OF THE ZONE

As mentioned in chapter 2, the rural area of study corresponds to the zones of Boyacá and Cundinamarca in the higher areas of the Andean region. This zone is located between 1,500 and 3,100 metres above sea level, and much of it resembles Bogotá in altitude (2,650 metres) and climatic conditions. The altitude of the defined strata differ, showing a bias of the lower stratum towards cooler zones, with a substantial proportion (30 per cent) located in the exceedingly cold zones at 2,800 metres or more above sea level. In contrast, the upper stratum is concentrated in the middle zones (40 per cent). This tight relation between altitude and socio-economic stratum is largely explained by land productivity in the different thermic floors. The exceedingly cold zones have very low productivity and normally are very difficult to reach. By contrast, as one descends, more adequate land for diverse farming is found, and thus productivity conditions, and income possibilities, improve.

This zone is reasonably accessible, and no general examples of extreme isolation are found. Recent years have shown a relative opening up of this area, owing to an intense government programme of penetration and integration roads. In general, the average travel time to the head city, trading place, or medical assistance centre in the township is nearly half an hour for a distance of about 7 kilometres, part of which is covered on foot.

The accessibility conditions are closely related to the socio-economic strata, since the strata are partly defined as a function of the degree of isolation. The low stratum is much more isolated than the upper stratum. This situation is not only determined by great distances, but by the difficult displacement conditions caused by the lack of roads. This is clearly seen in the differences in the access to roads. While in the lower stratum people must travel more than nine minutes to reach a road, in the upper stratum this takes only two minutes.

In relation to public services, the availability of health promoters is similar by stratum (about 54 per cent), but the availability of schools is different – 77 per cent of the communities in the lower stratum have schools, as against 94 per cent of those in the upper stratum. Table 8 presents the proportion of communities (clusters) with public services. Similarly, access to water supply and electricity is highly differentiated by socio-economic stratum. In the whole rural zone of our study, 50 per cent of the communities have access to a water supply system. This proportion is as low as 18 per cent in the lower stratum, whereas it is almost 87 per cent in the upper stratum. Water is a service that, as no other, determines quality of life and conditions of salubrity. Because it is closely related to infant mortality, it is particularly important to point out this difference, which produces a deep division between the lower and the upper strata.

Rural electrification has been a service with a high domiciliary coverage in Colombia, especially since the 1960s. According to the 1985 census, 41 per cent of rural dwellings in the country have this service, Boyacá (45 per cent) and Cundinamarca (51 per cent) being the states with the highest coverage. In the studied communities, nearly 87 per cent of villages have access to an electric power supply. Important differences are observed, by socio-economic stratum, similar to those observed in the access to water supply service. According to table 8, all the studied communities of the upper stratum have an energy system, while only 66 per cent of the lower stratum and 94 per cent of the middle stratum have it.

The community organization can be analysed from three different types of association schemes: public action boards, co-operatives and DRI[1] committees. Table 8 shows the proportion of communities with these types of organization. Public action boards, which are village organisms of reciprocal collaboration for attending to common necessities, and which in some cases carry out the infrastructure development programmes, are widespread in all communities (87 per

Table 8. Proportion of rural communities according to selected social indicators, by stratum (percentages)

Indicator	Stratum			Total
	Lower	Middle	Upper	
Public service				
School	77.0	89.8	94.1	86.9
Health promoter	48.3	61.5	51.7	53.8
Water supply	17.8	46.2	86.7	50.4
Electric power	65.8	94.0	100.0	86.5
Community organization				
Community action board	86.6	83.6	89.2	86.5
DRI committee	35.5	53.9	39.3	42.5
Co-operative	6.0	9.3	12.1	9.1
N	120	118	122	360

cent) with no differences by stratum. Co-operatives, which are associations performing more specific economic tasks, are present in only 9 per cent of the communities, with differences by stratum. While only 6 per cent of the villages in the lower stratum have co-operatives, 12 per cent of those in the upper stratum do. Finally, the DRI committees, which are mixed organizations with community members and state service companies promoting credit and technical assistance, are organized in 45 per cent of the studied villages. The middle stratum has the highest proportion of DRI committees, 54 per cent, whereas the lower and upper strata have 35 and 39 per cent respectively. This difference can be explained by government policies in the definition of the zones selected for coverage, this being an administrative decision based on the peasant economy conditions of the zones and not a consequence of the community development.

One important indicator of socio-economic level is given by the habitability of the housing stock. Two aspects can be distinguished: the first is related to the typologies and qualities of the dwellings, and the second to the supply of services.

Table 9 presents the distribution of dwellings by type. The main kind of dwelling is the self-standing unit house built of permanent materials and in generally good condition. Nearly 78 per cent of the dwellings of the studied zone are so classified. Next are the huts, which are not built with permanent materials, but which have a basic structure similar to the house: 21 per cent of the dwellings are of this type. The distribution is different by strata. In the lower stratum, 61 per cent of dwellings are houses and 38 per cent huts. In the upper stratum, by contrast, 92 per cent are houses and only 7 per cent huts. Although waste dwellings[2] are uncommon in rural areas, they represent 0.8 per cent of the dwellings in the study area. They were found mainly in the areas surrounding urban centres or on

Table 9. Distribution of rural dwellings according to type, by stratum (percentages)

Dwelling type	Stratum			
	Lower	Middle	Upper	Total
House	60.7	79.4	91.5	77.6
Hut	38.7	19.3	6.9	21.3
Waste dwelling	0.3	1.0	1.1	0.8
No report	0.3	0.3	0.5	0.3
Total	100.0	100.0	100.0	100.0
N	989	1,030	1,040	3,059

Table 10. Distribution of rural dwellings according to type of sanitary service, by stratum (percentages)

Sanitary service	Stratum			
	Lower	Middle	Upper	Total
Sewerage connection	3.3	3.0	23.9	10.3
Septic pit	9.0	23.6	36.1	23.2
Latrine	3.8	5.0	7.1	5.3
Absence	83.9	68.4	32.9	61.2
Total	100.0	100.0	100.0	100.0
N	989	1,030	1,040	3,059

road borders where the conditions of suburban development are a direct consequence of rapid urbanization.

The sewer system service to the dwellings gives an idea of living conditions and health standards as well as of attitudes and customs related to the use of modern conveniences. Table 10 shows the distribution of dwellings by sanitary type, and indicates that 10 per cent have connections to a sewer system, with wide differences by socio-economic stratum. The lower stratum has only 3 per cent of its dwellings connected to a system, while the upper one has 24 per cent. Although coverage for the upper stratum is still low, the difference from the lower stratum is substantial. The septic pit gives admissible hygiene and quality service conditions, a good substitute for a sewer system in rural areas. This category represents 23 per cent of the total dwellings, with important differences by socio-economic stratum: only 9 per cent of the lower stratum but 36 per cent of the higher are so classified. This means that 60 per cent of the upper stratum dwellings have adequate sanitary services, as against only 12 per cent of the lower and 26 per cent of the middle stratum.

The water closet is an alternative to the sewer system. Only 4 per cent of the dwellings in the lower stratum have water closets, compared to 7 per cent of the upper stratum. The differences between strata on access to any sanitary service are very important: 84 per cent of the dwellings from the lower stratum, 68 per cent of the middle, and 33 per cent of the upper stratum do not have a sanitary service.

Crowding, as an indicator of the habitability of a dwelling, can be analysed through the number of households sharing the dwelling and the number of persons per bedroom inside the dwelling. Data indicate that the number of households per dwelling is about 1.02, with no major differences by stratum. Similarly, relatively low crowding conditions are implied by the second indicator: 2.4 persons per bedroom, with some differences by socio-economic stratum – 2.6 in the lower and 2.2 in the upper stratum.

The characteristics of the zone under study indicate that the differences in socio-economic conditions are explained mainly by the existence and availability of basic infrastructures such as roads, electrification, and water supply, and by the quality of the dwellings. In this regard the differences between communities are so great that the activities and efforts of community organization show not much incidence in the socio-economic differentials between communities.

THE RURAL POPULATION

In this section we discuss the characteristics of the rural population living in the interviewed dwellings in terms of their living conditions and their productive and family organization.

Education. Access to the formal educational system determines important qualitative differences because of the cultural, economic, and ideological implications that this has for the population. A key variable reflecting the socio-economic stratification of a society is its educational level.

The illiteracy rate is 22.2 per cent for the population older than 5 years of age. In general, the region was found in better condition than the average rural zones of the country. For the latter areas, the 1985 census found an illiteracy rate of 29.9 per cent. Nevertheless, this rate is still far from the rate found in the same census for urban areas, 17.7 per cent. Important differences were found by socio-economic strata. While the population in the lower stratum had an illiteracy rate of 27.7 per cent, the rate for the upper stratum was about 17.5 per cent, very close to the average urban area rate. Although the rate for the lower stratum is higher than that for the upper stratum, it is lower than the national average for the rural areas. This indicates that our rural study zone has better literacy conditions than the average of the country, which may be due to the proximity of Bogotá.

The educational level is determined by attendance at a formal educational centre. Table 11 shows the attendance rates by age-groups. In general, the highest attendance rate is in the 10–14 age-group, in which 76.4 per cent of the total were studying. However, in the 5–9 age-group only 58 per cent were studying, with

Table 11. Rural school attendance rates, by age-group and stratum (percentages)

Age-group	Stratum		
	Lower	Middle	Upper
5–9	53.3	57.3	63.0
10–14	73.6	73.9	82.2
15–19	20.5	29.8	45.3
20–29	3.0	5.9	8.9
Over 29	1.3	0.6	0.5

32 per cent in the 15–19 age-group and a very low attendance after 19 years of age. These figures indicate that the population has a specific attendance pattern: they start school late and drop out very early. This pattern is observed in all three strata, with the upper strata always showing higher attendance rates. Two generalizations can be derived from the data on attendance behaviour: first, the late entrance of the population into school, and, second, the lack of success in holding the population within the educational system, especially in the secondary level, keeps educational attainment low for the rural population as a whole. This suggests that from an early age members of rural communities sacrifice investment in schooling to work on the family plot.

Examining attendance by sex, an interesting differential is found. Attendance in a formal school is consistently greater for women than for men for all age-groups. This can be attributed to the greater participation of men in work activities; from an early age they are socialized to assume productive responsibilities, even at the expense of their own schooling.

The educational profile for the population older than 5 years of age, presented in table 12, indicates that about 22.4 per cent of the population has no formal schooling, and that primary school was finished only by 28 per cent of the population, very few of whom went on to higher levels of education. Once again, there exist substantial differences by socio-economic strata: only 18.7 per cent of the lower stratum completed primary school, while 35.4 per cent of the upper stratum did so. A higher proportion of those who finished in the upper stratum went on to higher levels of education. That access to higher education is limited is evident in the extremely low proportions continuing on to secondary school. Only 2 per cent of the population finished secondary school, 0.7 per cent in the lower stratum, 1.6 per cent in the middle, and 3.7 per cent in the higher stratum.

Economic activities. Given the nature and organization of productive activities in the countryside, there is great variation in remuneration and work methods. We considered two types of labour participation. One is non-paid work in an agri-

Table 12. Distribution of the rural population of five years and older, by educational level and stratum (percentages)

Education	Stratum			
	Lower	Middle	Upper	Total
None	27.1	22.5	17.9	22.4
Incomplete primary	54.1	49.4	46.2	49.8
Complete primary	13.3	16.8	17.4	15.9
Incomplete secondary	4.7	9.5	14.3	9.6
Complete secondary	0.5	1.3	3.0	1.6
Superior or more	0.2	0.3	0.7	0.4
No information	0.1	0.2	0.5	0.3
Total	100.0	100.0	100.0	100.0
N	4,395	4,720	4,628	13,743

cultural or business family productive unit, a category that can incorporate family members working without remuneration. Second are jobs remunerated with money or in kind. This category does not consider the economic sector where the activity takes place, but only whether labour is exchanged for payment. Nevertheless, a great part of the productive activities, paid or family activities, is in agriculture. Paid activities refer here to the labour force sold to another agricultural producer. Non-paid activities refer to a household which constitutes a production unit in which its members do not receive payment for their work. In our analysis of the economic role of the household, family work in an agricultural enterprise is as important as family work in a family business. What is important for our purposes is that production requires the participation of various household members.

Table 13 shows the proportion of the population older than 10 years of age participating in paid and non-paid activities. About 57 per cent participate in non-paid activities, indicating a high contribution from the household members in these activities. Clear differences by stratum indicate that the degree to which the family labour force is involved in agricultural production is closely related to the socio-economic level. In the lower stratum 69 per cent participate, against only 45.1 per cent in the upper stratum. Participation in paid activities is lower than that observed in non-paid activities and is very similar by stratum, from 30.4 to 33.3 per cent in the lower and upper strata.

Differentials by sex show that participation in non-paid activities is higher among men than women in all strata. Although participation in non-paid activities decreases for both sexes, in the upper stratum the sex differential widens. The proportion is 75.9 per cent for men and 61.4 for women in the low stratum, whereas it is 51.2 per cent for men and 39 for women in the upper stratum.

Table 13. Proportion of the rural population of 10 years and older in productive activities, by stratum (percentages)

Productive activity	Stratum			Total
	Lower	Middle	Upper	
Non-paid	68.7	58.8	45.1	57.2
Paid	30.4	30.1	33.3	31.3
N	3,611	4,007	3,909	11,527

So far, a participation concept has been presented in which economic activity is defined in paid and non-paid terms. But real production conditions are a permanent combination of activities, such that the population simultaneously performs paid and non-paid family activities. In rural Colombia, households were the main production units, but subsistence activities were supplemented by the labour force sold by the household members. The participation rate of the population older than 10 years of age in a productive activity, paid or non-paid, is about 76 per cent in the lower stratum and 65 in the upper. However, a clear relation was found between the type of work and the living conditions represented by the stratum. Although participation in only non-paid family activities is the norm for all the strata, it is much more important in the lower stratum, 45 per cent, compared to the upper one, 31 per cent. Similarly, the combination of paid and non-paid activities is more important in the lower stratum, 24 per cent, than in the upper stratum, 14 per cent. The remarkable difference by stratum in the participation in only paid work balanced this, 19 per cent in the upper stratum and 7.5 per cent in the lower stratum. Thus, the proportion of the population in paid activities is greater the higher the stratum.

HOUSEHOLD PRODUCTIVE STRUCTURE

The organization of the household for production determines the production typology, which has implications for the economic conditions of the area. In contrast to the urban areas, the dwellings in the rural areas are part of the exploitation unit. Table 14 presents the distribution of households by tenancy relationship. Ownership is the predominant category, about 74 per cent, which is closely related to the fact that this rural area is predominantly a region of small-holdings. The next category is rented, 9.5 per cent, which can be associated with a non-traditional production type since the ability to produce a monetary surplus is a necessity to pay the rent. By stratum, ownership is more common in the lower stratum, 78 per cent, than in the upper one, 64 per cent. This indicates that ownership does not necessarily determine the living conditions of the household. It determines ownership of the basic means of agricultural production, but it does not guarantee the capacity to produce a surplus for commercialization.

Table 14. Distribution of rural households according to type of dwelling tenancy, by stratum (percentages)

Tenancy	Stratum			
	Lower	Middle	Upper	Total
Owner	77.7	79.4	64.1	73.6
Tenant	6.4	6.8	15.3	9.5
Partner	4.5	2.9	2.4	3.3
In pawn	0.5	0.1	0.2	0.3
In administration	5.9	5.3	5.1	5.2
Free	2.7	4.1	3.9	5.3
Other	2.3	1.4	4.5	2.8
Total	100.0	100.0	100.0	100.0
N	1,011	1,055	1,067	3,133

The other forms of tenancy, partnership and pawn relations, represent traditional production conditions. In the latter, products are exchanged for work. These forms are not predominant in the study areas – only 3.6 per cent of the households belong to these two categories.

The main source of household support is closely related to tenancy relations. Table 15 presents the classification of the households and distinguishes between support from subsistence activities, agricultural activities, non-agricultural activities, wages, and payments or other revenues. The main sources of household support are family agricultural activities (36.7 per cent), subsistence activities (23.2 per cent), and wages (20.1 per cent). The clearest differences by stratum are between household support from subsistence activities and wages. The first source of support prevails among the households in the lower stratum, about 37 per cent of which live off subsistence – that is, off activities without a commercial surplus and with low productive conditions – and only 12 per cent depend mainly on wages. In the upper stratum, on the contrary, the predominant source of support is wages, 31 per cent, whereas only 12 per cent of the households live off subsistence. This shows the differences existing in the structure of production between the socio-economic strata.

Women's Socio-economic Characteristics

This section deals with the socio-economic characteristics of the urban and rural women at the time of the interview. A cross-section static analysis gives us a global view of women's backgrounds and their current conditions as a basis for the dynamic analysis of women's demographic behaviour over the life-course.

Table 15. Distribution of rural households according to main source of support, by stratum (percentages)

Support source	Stratum			
	Lower	Middle	Upper	Total
Subsistence production	36.6	21.4	12.3	23.2
Family exploitation	36.0	44.3	29.9	36.7
Livestock exploitation	3.0	3.0	3.7	3.3
Partnership agricultural exploitation	6.8	7.8	4.7	6.4
Trade	0.5	2.1	6.9	3.2
Industry	1.8	0.6	1.6	1.3
Services	0.1	0.9	3.3	1.4
Salaries	11.8	16.6	31.4	20.1
Rents or pensions	2.0	2.1	2.0	2.0
Total	100.0	100.0	100.0	100.0
N	1,011	1,055	1,067	3,133

Origin and Migration

Urban and rural women have parents predominantly of rural origin. About 45 per cent of the urban women and more than 90 per cent of rural women have parents of rural origin. Although there are no differences between younger and older cohorts, there is a relationship between parents' origins and women's stratum, especially in the urban area. There, about 57 per cent of the women in the lower stratum have parents of rural origin, whereas only 15 per cent of those in the upper stratum do. Thus, urban origin is predominant among parents of the urban women in the upper stratum, but rural origin prevails among parents of the urban women in the lower stratum and among parents of all rural women.

The predominantly rural origin of the parents is a determinant characteristic of the predominantly rural origin of the interviewed women in the rural area and in the urban lower stratum. Table 16 presents the distribution of urban and rural women by origin, cohort and stratum. About 60 per cent of the younger and 83 per cent of the older urban women are migrants, of whom more than 80 per cent come from rural areas. This is an expression of the low stability of the population in Bogotá over the last 30 years, during which the city has been subject to a marked process of immigration from other parts of the country. Rural women, by contrast, are highly stable: about half of them still live in the same rural place where they were born.

In both areas and in both cohorts, there exists a positive correlation between origin and stratum.[3] The higher the stratum, the higher the proportion of women of urban origin. Thus, not only is the proportion of migrants in urban areas

Table 16. Distribution of women, by origin, cohort, and stratum (percentages)

Origin	Younger cohort				Older cohort			
	Lower	Middle	Upper	Total	Lower	Middle	Upper	Total
Urban area								
Urban native	30.6	44.3	46.3	40.1	14.1	15.7	31.3	16.8
Urban	7.4	13.6	17.1	11.3	3.1	10.8	28.4	10.7
Rural	62.0	43.2	36.6	48.6	82.0	73.5	40.3	72.6
Total	100.0	100.0	100.0	100.0	100.0	100.0	100.0	100.0
N	258	188	132	578	164	186	145	496
Rural area								
Urban	3.5	6.8	13.4	8.6	1.6	3.5	6.8	4.0
Rural	39.2	39.8	55.2	45.6	37.2	29.7	49.2	38.7
Rural native	57.3	53.4	31.4	45.8	61.2	66.8	44.0	57.3
Total	100.0	100.0	100.0	100.0	100.0	100.0	100.0	100.0
N	145	180	208	533	179	204	195	578

higher the lower the stratum, but the proportion of migrants from rural areas is higher the lower the stratum – clear evidence of the correlation between origin and living conditions in the urban area. Yet number of years of residence in Bogotá is not correlated with socio-economic stratum. Urban women in all three strata show similar migration patterns – about 85.5 per cent of the younger cohort and 94.6 per cent of the older cohort are migrants of more than five years ago.

However, one important change in migration patterns emerges when one looks at origin controlling by time of residence in Bogotá. Recent migration comes mostly from other urban areas (cities) instead of rural zones. This is an important change in the migration flows to Bogotá.

Education

Independent of the stratum, we find that the level of education of the younger cohort is higher than that of the older women, and that in turn is higher than those of their parents. We find, in general, that across cohorts and strata, fathers have had uniformly more education than the mothers in both urban and rural areas. In the urban area, however, differences in educational attainments between the younger women and their mothers show no variations by stratum. For the older urban cohort and both rural cohorts the differences in education with their mothers is greater the higher the stratum. These data show a broadening of

Table 17. Distribution of women by level of education, cohort, and stratum (percentages)

Education	Younger cohort				Older cohort			
	Lower	Middle	Upper	Total	Lower	Middle	Upper	Total
Urban area								
None	3.0	3.3	1.7	3.0	28.7	11.4	3.7	14.6
Primary	55.5	25.6	11.1	34.2	64.6	57.2	7.5	54.2
Secondary	40.1	53.1	24.1	46.6	6.1	29.8	56.0	26.9
University or more	1.4	18.0	63.1	16.2	0.6	1.6	32.8	4.3
Total	100.0	100.0	100.0	100.0	100.0	100.0	100.0	100.0
N	258	188	132	578	164	186	145	496
Years of school	5.9	8.1	11.7	7.7	2.9	5.2	10.6	5.2
Rural area								
None	13.3	9.6	8.3	10.1	47.8	36.4	23.3	35.6
Primary	77.6	77.5	67.4	73.5	49.5	60.6	67.9	59.4
Secondary	9.1	12.9	22.8	15.8	2.7	3.0	8.3	4.8
University or more	—	—	1.5	0.6	—	—	0.5	0.2
Total	100.0	100.0	100.0	100.0	100.0	100.0	100.0	100.0
N	145	180	208	533	179	204	195	578
Years of school	3.0	3.4	4.3	3.6	1.4	1.6	2.6	1.8

educational possibilities for the different strata in the urban area, and a strata-differentiated increase in access to the educational system in rural areas.

Table 17 presents the distribution of women by level of education, cohort, stratum, and location. The increase in access to basic education from the older to the younger urban and rural cohorts is clear from the table. Although the urban–rural differential in access to basic education decreased from the older to the younger cohort, it is still important. The proportion of urban women with no education was only 3.0 and 14.6 per cent in the younger and older cohorts. For the rural area, those figures were 10.1 and 35.6 per cent. Since rural origin prevails among urban women in the lower stratum, high access to basic education in all urban strata contradicts the expectation that urban women of rural origin usually have a lower access to the educational system than urban women of urban origin.

Comparing the educational profiles within areas we observe a large difference between cohorts, evidence of a substantial change. High-school education was the modal education level for the younger urban cohort, with an average of 7.7

years of schooling completed. The older urban cohort shows 54.2 per cent in elementary school and an average of 5.2 years of schooling.[4] However, by stratum, the profile is different. For example, the younger urban cohort in the upper stratum is outstanding, with about 63.1 per cent of the women having had superior education, while those in the lower stratum have only 1.4 per cent at that level. The younger urban women in the upper stratum have on average 11.7 years of schooling, whereas those in the lower stratum have only 5.9 years. The differentials are similar for the older urban cohort: 10.6 years of schooling for women in the upper stratum and only 2.9 for women in the lower stratum. This sharp differential in educational attainment between urban women in the different socio-economic strata has important implications for their productive and reproductive behaviours, since it is well known – and this was documented in chapter 2 – that education is a variable highly correlated with fertility and female labour-force participation. Stated differently, education shapes decisively the life-course of women.

In the rural area there has also been an improvement in educational attainment, although the levels of the younger cohort are still low. The average years of schooling increase from 1.8 in the older cohort to 3.6 in the younger. By stratum, the profile is not as different as in the urban area. Rural women in the younger upper stratum average 4.3 years of schooling; those in the lower stratum average 3.0. For the older cohort the figures are 2.6 and 1.4 years respectively. Thus, levels of education in the rural area are lower than primary school, even for the younger women in the upper socio-economic stratum. These low levels of educational attainment among rural women affect their productive and reproductive behaviour and differentiate it from that of urban women through a qualitative difference in access to information, and the capacity to act upon it.

The differential educational levels by stratum in the urban area and the low levels obtained in all strata in the rural area are related to the high drop-out rates observed, even during elementary school, and to the poor access to secondary or superior education. Table 18 presents the access and drop-out rates for different levels of education by cohort and strata for both urban and rural women. Urban data show that although access to primary education is high and independent of the stratum, drop-out rates are closely related to the stratum. About 97.3 per cent (71.1 per cent) of the younger (older) cohort in the urban low stratum started primary school. However, of those only 75 per cent (32 per cent) finished it. In the upper stratum, about 98 per cent started and almost 96 per cent finished primary school. Similarly, access to secondary or higher education in urban areas is related to the socio-economic stratum. Although 92 per cent (96 per cent) of those younger (older) urban women in the upper stratum who finished primary school began secondary school, only 69 per cent (30 per cent) of the younger (older) cohort in the lower stratum did so. At the secondary level, drop-out rates are highly differentiated by stratum. Almost 90 per cent of the younger cohort in the

Table 18. Female access and drop-out rates of formal education, by cohort and stratum (percentages)

Education	Younger cohort				Older cohort			
	Lower	Middle	Upper	Total	Lower	Middle	Upper	Total
Urban area								
Primary								
Access	97.3	97.3	98.4	97.4	71.1	91.9	98.5	90.3
Drop-out	24.7	5.6	2.5	11.3	67.9	28.2	5.3	33.9
Secondary								
Access[a]	69.3	85.1	92.3	81.5	29.5	51.6	96.0	55.8
Drop-out	64.9	49.0	11.1	49.0	84.6	76.2	32.5	65.9
Rural area								
Primary								
Access[a]	91.7	94.4	94.7	93.8	63.2	71.1	82.6	72.5
Drop-out	66.4	60.7	42.1	54.9	81.7	81.0	69.2	76.6
Secondary								
Access	29.5	34.8	44.2	38.6	23.8	23.1	34.7	29.2
Drop-out	64.3	72.4	78.3	74.8	66.7	62.5	66.7	65.6

a. Of those who finish primary school.

upper stratum complete their secondary schooling; only 35 per cent of those in the lower stratum finish. Thus, these differentiated access and drop-out rates determine the differentials in the observed levels of education between women in the different urban strata.

Rural results are similar but with lower access and higher drop-out rates. Although 93.8 per cent of the younger rural cohort and 72.5 per cent of the rural older cohort start primary school, only 45 and 27 per cent complete it. Among those who finish elementary school, only 39 per cent (29 per cent) of the younger (older) cohort start secondary school: of those, only 75 per cent (65 per cent) finish it. In short, high drop-out rates, even from primary school, and poor access to secondary education explain the low educational attainment of rural women.

Thus, educational profiles clearly show substantial improvements in educational attainments from the younger to the older urban and rural cohorts. The low levels among the younger urban women in the lower stratum are related to the low access to secondary and post-secondary schooling. The low levels still observed among the younger rural women are mainly due to the inability of the educational system to retain the students at the primary level as well as to the low access to higher educational levels.

Table 19. Proportion of women currently and ever occupied, by cohort and stratum (percentages)

Activity	Younger cohort				Older cohort			
	Lower	Middle	Upper	Total	Lower	Middle	Upper	Total
Urban area								
Paid work								
Ever	75.6	85.8	84.4	82.5	75.6	71.4	74.6	72.7
Currently	28.1	43.8	67.0	41.0	38.4	37.1	43.0	38.0
Rural area								
Paid work								
Ever	41.4	46.1	61.5	50.8	34.1	32.3	48.2	38.2
Currently	14.6	14.9	20.7	17.1	6.0	4.5	6.2	5.5
Non-paid work								
Ever								
Farm	54.5	48.9	42.3	47.8	57.7	56.6	54.3	56.2
Plot[a]	62.1	51.7	44.7	51.8	67.6	58.7	53.8	59.9
Currently								
Farm	39.6	37.6	28.4	34.5	35.8	40.3	29.2	36.0
Plot[a]	52.8	46.4	34.6	43.5	54.4	45.8	34.9	44.8

a. Refers to production only for subsistence.

Labour-force Participation

Work experience in the labour market should be analysed controlling by the age differences between cohorts, since it defines stages in the life-cycle not comparable with each other. Table 19 presents the proportion of women who have ever worked and are currently working by cohort and stratum for urban and rural areas. Urban and rural results indicate an increase between cohorts in the proportion of women who have ever worked in paid activities. About 73 per cent of the older urban cohort have ever had a paid job, whereas 82.5 per cent of the younger cohort had had one by the time of the survey. For the rural area the differences are even greater, 38 and 51 per cent. Although this is so in all urban and rural strata, the major differences are among women in the upper stratum, who consistently show greater work experience. Given the distinct life-cycle stages of the two cohorts – an age difference of almost 20 years – those results permit us to foresee significant increases in the participation of the younger cohorts.

Rural productive activities include, besides paid work, such agricultural family non-paid activities as farm and plot work.[5] It is clear from the data that, independent of the cohort and the strata, a high proportion of rural women have performed non-paid activities: about 50 per cent have worked on a family farm or family plot. However, the proportion of women with this work experience is lower in the younger than in the older cohort, especially in the upper stratum. This could be the result of the different stages at which they find themselves in their life-cycles. However, since the proportion of younger women with experience in paid work has increased, this could also suggest that younger rural women are moving away from non-paid agricultural activities to paid activities (in agriculture or otherwise).

In the urban area, the current level of participation in paid work is highly differentiated by socio-economic stratum among the younger cohort, but not among women in the older cohort, nor among women in the rural area. While the older urban cohort has rates of labour participation of between 38 and 43 per cent, the younger ones have 28 per cent in the lower stratum and 67 per cent in the higher stratum. In the rural area, only about 17 per cent of the younger cohort and 5 per cent of the younger and older cohort were currently working in a paid job. Although there is very low female participation of both rural cohorts in paid activities, almost half of them were engaged in plot activities at the time of the survey, and about 35 per cent were working on a family farm. Thus, the tendency in most of the formal employment studies not to consider plot and family activities as economically productive activities underestimates female labour-force participation in rural areas. These should be considered as productive activities not only because of the contribution they make to household production for subsistence, but because women themselves recognize and value those activities as being productive. Chapter 5 covers these considerations in depth through the analysis of the perception women have of domestic and productive work.

The classification by occupation of those urban women who were working in a paid job at the moment of the survey indicates that about 45 per cent of the younger cohort were professional and 38 per cent were sales and services workers. Among women in the older cohort, only 20 per cent were professional and about 61 per cent were sales and services workers. These differences are even sharpr between women in the upper stratum. This suggests a very important qualitative change in the productive activities of urban cohorts, which is surely related to the observed improvements in their educational attainments. In the rural area, more than half (55 per cent) of the women working in a paid job at the time of the survey were services workers, which includes schoolteachers and nurses, and only about 10 per cent were agricultural workers. This low participation in agricultural activities reflects the fact that most of the rural women's agriculture activities on family farms or plots were non-paid.

The availability of occupational histories allows us to make some inferences about occupational patterns and mobility. Since occupational patterns are analysed in the next chapter, we consider here only occupational mobility. The number of paid jobs held during a lifetime demonstrates the low occupational mobility of both urban and rural women. About half of the urban women and 70 per cent of the rural women have had only one paid job.[6] This proportion is even higher among women in the lower stratum. The changes in occupation among urban women are related to the type of occupation. Thus, we find that women who start their working life in professional or technical occupations or as administrative officials do not show a change in occupation. By contrast, women who started their working life in agricultural activities have largely moved to sales and services. This mobility must correspond to the immigrant women who started working in the countryside and whose first job was therefore in agricultural activities.

The above general description of the work variables leads to the conclusion that there exists a clear tendency towards a greater labour-force participation among younger cohorts, irrespective of rural–urban residence. In part this reflects increases in the opportunity cost of women's time as a consequence of the great improvements in their educational attainments, especially among urban women. Not only have the participation rates increased, but there has been a movement from the older to the younger cohort toward more qualified occupations in the urban areas and away from family agricultural activities in the rural areas.

Marital Status, Fertility, and Use of Family Planning

Differences in the reproductive cycle between cohorts do not allow us directly to compare them in terms of demographic variables. Therefore, the analysis here refers to the differential behaviour by stratum within each group of women. Table 20 presents some fertility-related indicators at the time of the interview, such as the proportion of single women, the mean number of children ever born, and the proportion of women who have ever used family-planning methods.

Among women in the younger urban cohort there is a clear differential behaviour in marriage patterns between urban and rural areas, and by stratum within each area. That the proportion of single women is higher in the urban areas (25 per cent) than in the rural areas (17 per cent) suggests later marriage patterns among urban women. However, the behaviour is different by stratum. Whereas almost 50 per cent of the younger urban cohort in the upper stratum were still single at the time of the interview, only about 11 per cent of those urban women in the lower stratum were. In the rural area, on the contrary, the proportion of single women in the younger cohort is higher among women in the lower stratum (21.4 per cent) than among women in the upper stratum (14 per cent). This suggests not only different marriage[7] patterns between urban and rural areas but also different marriage patterns by stratum within areas.[8] There is, however, a high stability in both urban and rural unions. About 98 per cent of the women in the younger urban and rural cohorts have been married only once. Among women in the older cohort, the proportions are 93 per cent in the urban areas and 96 per cent in the rural areas.

Retrospective fertility data confirm a clearly differential behaviour by stratum

Table 20. Selected fertility indicators, by cohort and stratum

Area	Younger cohort				Older cohort			
	Lower	Middle	Upper	Total	Lower	Middle	Upper	Total
Urban area								
Single (%)	11.6	25.7	49.2	25.3	8.0	4.8	2.7	5.3
Mean no. of children ever born	2.3	1.5	0.8	1.6	6.1	4.6	3.3	4.8
Used family planning (%)[a]	77.2	70.1	47.4	68.2	66.3	60.4	61.0	62.5
Used family planning (%)[a]	86.9	90.6	88.1	89.9	67.9	64.2	73.6	66.2
Rural area								
Single (%)	21.4	17.2	13.9	17.1	13.1	7.5	9.2	10.0
Mean no. of children ever born	3.0	2.9	2.8	2.9	6.1	6.4	5.8	6.1
Used family planning (%)[a]	34.7	39.8	55.8	44.7	32.4	32.8	36.9	34.1
Used family planning (%)[a]	42.5	47.3	63.1	52.6	36.3	34.9	40.7	39.4

a. Proportion of ever-married women.

and area. The mean number of children ever born by the time of the interview is lower in urban areas, and lower for the upper stratum. Younger urban women have had on average 1.6 children, whereas younger rural women have already had 2.9 children. Among women in the older cohort, the mean number of children ever born is 4.8 in the urban area and 6.1 in the rural area. The differentials by stratum are sharp in the urban area and almost non-existent in the rural area. Younger urban women in the upper stratum have given birth to less than one child on average, whereas their counterparts in the lower stratum have had more than two. For urban women in the older cohort the differentials by stratum are similar: women in the upper stratum have had almost half the number of children of women in the lower stratum (3.3 and 6.1 respectively). These fertility differentials are certainly related to the differences in marriage patterns suggested above. The observed fertility is the result of marriage and marital fertility behaviours.

Fertility behaviour, however, is also affected by illegitimate births when those are a significant proportion of total births. Although legal and consensual unions were always considered as marriage (or union), we still observe a high proportion of single women with children, especially in the rural area. Table 21 shows the distribution of single women by number of children ever born. About 16 and 26 per cent of single women in the younger and older urban cohorts have had at least one child. Among the single rural women, the proportions are as high as 40 and 50 per cent among the younger and older cohort respectively.

Table 21. Distribution of single women, by children ever born, cohort, and stratum (percentages)

Area	Younger cohort				Older cohort			
	Lower	Middle	Upper	Total	Lower	Middle	Upper	Total
Urban area								
None	73.3	85.4	89.2	83.6	75.0	72.7	80.0	74.2
1	16.7	12.5	10.8	13.5	25.0	18.2	8.0	18.6
2 or more	10.0	2.1	—	2.9	—	9.1	12.0	7.2
Total	100.0	100.0	100.0	100.0	100.0	100.0	100.0	100.0
N	258	188	132	578	164	186	145	496
Rural area								
None	45.2	67.7	69.0	60.4	28.0	60.0	77.8	51.7
1	25.8	16.1	20.7	20.9	12.0	13.3	5.6	10.3
2 or more	29.0	16.2	10.3	18.7	60.0	26.7	16.6	38.0
Total	100.0	100.0	100.0	100.0	100.0	100.0	100.0	100.0
N	145	180	208	533	179	204	195	578

Non-marital fertility also is related to a woman's social stratum: the lower the stratum the higher the proportion of single women with children. For example, among younger single rural women in the lower stratum, almost 55 per cent have already had at least one child, against nearly 30 per cent of single women in the upper stratum. This could be related to the environment and activities performed by urban and rural women in the lower stratum, which are mostly household activities as domestic employees. It is also related to the attitude of rural women towards use of family planning among single women. Our ethnographic work on women's perceptions (chapter 5) showed that all rural women, and especially those in the lower stratum, oppose the use of birth control by single women, place a very strong value on maternity, and have a quite negative view on abortion. Thus, women's perceptions on these themes help to account for the high proportion of rural single women with children.

Fertility behaviour is also affected by family-planning use. Table 20 shows the proportion of total women and women who have ever been married who have used family-planning methods. It is clear that there has been a significant increase from the older to the younger cohorts in the proportion of women who have used birth control in both urban and rural areas. While 66 per cent of the ever-married older urban cohort have used at least one method, about 90 per cent of those in the younger cohort have done so, even considering their shorter reproductive span. A similar increase is found in the rural area. About 39 per cent of ever-married women in the older cohort have used family-planning methods, compared with almost 53 per cent in the younger cohort.

Since nuptiality patterns differ between areas and by stratum, and since family planning in Colombia is highly correlated with marital status, the difference between family-planning use by stratum among all women may give a biased picture of the situation. Among ever-married women, there is a positive correlation between use of birth control and stratum in the rural area, but not in the urban area. About 88 per cent of those ever-married urban women in the younger cohort upper stratum have used family planning at some time. Similarly, about 87 per cent of those younger urban women in the lower stratum have practised contraception. However, whereas 63 per cent of rural younger women in the upper stratum have used birth control, only 42.5 per cent of younger rural women in the lower stratum have done so. This could be explained by the high accessibility of family-planning methods in urban areas, independent of social strata. In rural areas, however, the higher the stratum, the higher the accessibility conditions of the zone, and hence the greater the accessibility of family-planning methods.

Not only the prevalence of family-planning use but also the effectiveness of the methods used affects fertility levels. Table 22 presents the distribution of women who have ever used birth control by first method used. It is evident that, independent of the stratum, younger cohorts have started their family control with mod-

Table 22. Distribution of women,[a] by first method used, cohort, and stratum (percentages)

Method	Younger cohort				Older cohort			
	Lower	Middle	Upper	Total	Lower	Middle	Upper	Total
Urban area								
Pill	44.0	44.0	50.0	45.1	17.6	35.9	29.3	27.7
IUD	31.0	33.1	27.8	31.0	30.6	23.5	4.5	20.2
Sterilization	4.5	0.8	—	2.5	8.3	1.8	3.4	4.5
Other modern	8.0	7.6	7.9	7.9	3.7	8.7	22.4	10.9
Traditional	12.5	14.5	14.3	13.5	39.8	30.1	40.4	36.7
Total	100.0	100.0	100.0	100.0	100.0	100.0	100.0	100.0
N	258	188	132	578	164	186	145	496
Rural area								
Pill	32.0	33.3	37.9	35.3	11.9	16.7	16.7	15.2
IUD	32.0	27.8	29.3	29.4	25.4	22.7	20.8	22.8
Sterilization	6.0	4.2	2.6	3.8	28.8	21.2	29.2	26.4
Other modern	6.0	11.1	12.1	10.5	1.7	6.1	6.9	5.2
Traditional	24.0	23.6	18.1	21.0	32.7	33.3	26.4	30.4
Total	100.0	100.0	100.0	100.0	100.0	100.0	100.0	100.0
N	145	180	208	533	179	204	195	578

a. Women who have ever used family-planning methods.

ern and effective methods, such as the pill and IUD, whereas a high proportion of women in the older cohort started with traditional methods. Most of the younger urban women started using birth control with the pill (45 per cent) or the IUD (31 per cent), and only 13 per cent started with traditional methods. Almost 37 per cent of the older urban women, on the other hand, started using traditional methods. Given the different life-cycle between cohorts, we observe a higher proportion of women in the older cohort who have used sterilization as first method. The proportion is significant among rural women (26.4 per cent), where family size is higher, suggesting a desire to control effectively the number of children they have. That is, a high proportion of older rural women started family planning after they had achieved their desired family size, using the most effective birth-control method, sterilization. This could be related to the time when family-planning programmes reach rural areas and to the positive attitude of rural women to using birth control after the family size has been achieved. This position became clear from the qualitative field-work on women's perceptions of their lives (the results of which are presented in chapter 5).

Table 23. Mean number of children ever born, by education, origin, and work experience by cohort

Characteristic	Urban area		Rural area	
	Younger	Older	Younger	Older
Education				
None	2.5	5.6	3.3	6.7
Incomplete primary	2.4	5.6	3.2	6.0
Complete primary	2.4	5.2	2.7	5.6
Incomplete secondary	1.7	3.9	2.0	3.6
Complete secondary or more	0.9	3.2	a	a
Origin				
Urban	1.6	4.5	N.A.	N.A.
Rural	2.0	5.3	N.A.	N.A.
Work experience (paid job)				
None	3.8	5.3	2.9	6.5
Some	2.9	4.5	2.8	5.4

a. Included in the category incomplete secondary.

Some Interrelationships

Socio-economic and demographic variables are generally interrelated. As stated in chapter 2, education, female labour-force participation, origin, and place of residence are related to fertility levels. Thus, we try here to develop static and first approximation to those interrelationships from a cross-section point of view, that is, from women's data at the moment of the survey.

Table 23 shows the mean number of children ever born by level of education, origin, and work experience in a paid job for both urban and rural areas. There is a clear and monotone negative relationship between educational level and fertility. However, the data suggests that the relationship is stronger at levels above completed primary school, especially among urban women. Younger urban women with no education or those with a completed elementary-school education bear an average of 2.4 children, whereas those with an incomplete secondary education have 1.7 and those with completed secondary or more bear less than one child on average. Thus, since the most significant improvements in education have been observed among urban women, they, and especially those in the upper stratum, have benefited in terms of fertility behaviour as a result of their observed increases in education above primary level.

Fertility by origin is presented only for urban women since, as we mentioned before, more than 90 per cent of rural women are of rural origin. Among urban women, origin is negatively related to fertility. Older urban women of urban origin have had on average 4.5 children, whereas those of rural origin have borne 5.3. Since urban women usually have higher access to the educational system than rural women, this negative relationship between origin and fertility could be an indirect effect of educational attainment. This hypothesis is considered in the next chapter, where we examine the determinants of family formation in a multivariate framework.

Female labour-force experience is negatively related to the number of children, especially in the urban area. Those women who have worked in a paid job have lower fertility than those who have never worked. This finding is very common in developed and developing countries, especially in urban areas. Urban women in the older cohort with work experience bore an average of 4.5 children, while those with no experience had 5.3 children by the date of the interview. The older rural cohort with work experience had had 5.4 and those with no experience had 6.5 children. The younger rural cohort, on the other hand, do not show differentials by work experience. This could be related to the compatibility of productive and reproductive roles of women in rural areas and to the fact that rural women in general tend to use birth control after they have formed their desired family size. This position was evident from the analysis of women's attitudes and perceptions based on the ethnographic work to be presented in chapter 5.

Since fertility and female work relationship is not unidirectional but rather complex, we also look at the proportion of women currently working by number of children ever born, current marital status, and education. Table 24 gives the results. Women's educational level shows a direct relationship to their labour-force participation, suggesting a higher opportunity cost of women's time the higher the level of education. Higher educational attainments favour participation in productive paid activities in both urban and rural areas. About 30 per cent of those urban women in the younger cohort with no education were working in paid jobs, whereas 43 per cent of those with completed primary education and 60 per cent of those with completed secondary or more were doing so. Although the relationship is not monotonic in the rural area, there is a clear difference in higher participation between those with incomplete secondary or more education and those with no education at all.

Current marital status approximates the presence of a mate (or spouse) in the household. This variable clearly shows the relationship between forming a family and reluctance to participate in the labour force. Urban women without a spouse – single women – show rates of participation remarkably higher than those of married women in both urban and rural areas. For example, in the urban younger cohort the difference in participation is 78 per cent for single women and 29 per cent for ever-married women. In the older cohort the differentials are in

Table 24. Proportion of women working by education, marital status, and children ever born, by cohort

Characteristic	Urban area		Rural area	
	Younger	Older	Younger	Older
Education				
None	29.6	36.0	51.5	43.4
Incomplete primary	42.9	39.2	48.0	31.8
Complete primary	43.1	33.1	44.7	31.9
Incomplete secondary	50.1	51.0	65.0	83.9
Complete secondary	60.3	67.6	a	a
or more				
Marital status				
Single	77.9	53.7	53.8	58.6
Ever-married	28.9	34.9	50.2	36.0
Number of children ever born				
0	69.4	42.9	53.0	51.4
1–2	34.9	36.5	57.1	52.2
3–4	35.2	41.1	48.0	55.1
5 or more	25.5	38.6	44.6	31.2

a. Included in the category incomplete secondary.

the same direction, but with lower levels. Thus, the presence of a spouse in the household diminishes female participation in economic activities.

The relationship between the number of children and labour participation is inverse in the urban area, showing the restriction that the presence of children has on the possibility of women participating in an economically productive activity. Urban women with no children show participation rates superior to those observed among urban women with children. Thus, about 69.4 per cent of those younger urban women with no children were working in productive activities, whereas only 25 per cent of those younger women with five or more children were working. For urban women with no children, participation is higher in the younger than in the older cohort. For urban women with children, participation is greater in the older than in the younger cohort and is independent of the number of children. Since children belonging to women in the older cohort may in general be over ten years old, the differentials in participation suggest that the restriction of children on female work is more related to children's age than to their number.

Although participation rates in the urban area by length of residence in Bogotá are not presented, they revealed sharp differences. Recent migrants, with less than five years in Bogotá, showed lower participation rates, 32 against 44 per cent in the younger cohort and 18 against 41 per cent in the older cohort. This could be related to better opportunities the longer the time of residence in Bogotá, or to higher educational attainments obtained once they arrive in the urban area.

In general, we find from the analysis of labour participation that the productive role of women is affected by family-forming aspects, since having children and a mate diminishes female labour-force participation.

Summary

The urban study has as a setting the city of Bogotá, capital of Colombia. The rural areas make reference to the rural zones of Cundinamarca and Boyacá, states located in the same geographic and cultural zone as Bogotá. This rural area accounts for almost 80 per cent of the total migrants to Bogotá. Both urban and rural settings have good access to public services such as education, health, roads, water supply, sewerage, and electrification, better than the average for the entire country. However, the characteristics of the zones indicate that differences by socio-economic strata within each zone are explained mainly by the existence and availability of the basic infrastructure and by the quality of the dwellings.

Although the population of Bogotá has relatively high levels of education in relation to all of Colombia, there exists a low access to superior levels of education. The rural zone of study showed good access to primary education, but an incapacity of the system to hold the population at that level, along with a very low access to secondary education. This partly explains the relatively low levels of educational attainment among the rural population. The economic base of Bogotá makes it a metropolitan urban centre with a large tertiary sector. In the rural zones, the participation of the population in agricultural non-paid family activities prevails, and the main source of household support comes from a combination of family agricultural activities and activities for subsistence and wages, but there are notable differences by strata.

A low proportion of the urban women studied are native to Bogotá, and the origin of the migrant women is predominantly rural, especially among women in the lower stratum. The majority of rural women, on the other hand, are native, and a high proportion of them still live in the same place of birth. This is not surprising since, given the characteristics of the rural area, the population living there would correspond to those who have not migrated to Bogotá.

A comparison of educational profiles among urban women indicates a substantial increase in the educational level from the older to the younger cohort: the younger cohort is predominantly high-school educated, whereas in the older cohort completion of primary school is the modal education level. However, by strata the profile is different; among the younger urban cohort in the upper stratum a high proportion have undertaken higher education. Although educational profiles for women in the rural area also show an increase in access to basic education, the low levels of education obtained by both cohorts are related to the high drop-out rates observed, even during the primary years, and to poor access to secondary or higher education. Even for the younger rural cohort we observe average levels of education below the primary.

Female labour-force participation increased from the older to the younger cohort in both urban and rural areas, and for all strata. This behaviour is more important if we consider the age and life-cycle differences between the groups. The younger cohort will most probably increase its labour-force participation, thus widening the differences between cohorts. It does not appear that the higher participation of the younger cohort results from greater opportunity costs of women's time as a consequence of their substantial improvements in education. Not only have the participation rates increased, but there has been a movement from the older to the younger cohort, toward more qualified occupations in the urban areas and away from family agricultural activities in the rural area.

Marital status at the time of the interview suggests different marriage patterns between urban and rural areas and between socio-economic strata within each area. Given the influence of nuptiality on fertility, this is certainly related to the clear differential behaviours by stratum and area in retrospective fertility. Similarly, fertility behaviour is affected by the significant increase observed from the older to the younger cohort in the proportion of women who have ever used family-planning methods. Its effect is even more important if one considers that there has been an increase in the use of more effective and modern methods, such as the pill and IUD. This increase in birth control in both urban and rural areas is surely a consequence of both the higher levels of education of the population, which led them to accept its use, and higher coverage by family-planning pro-grammes, especially in rural areas. This is confirmed by the fact that rural women in the lower stratum are the ones with the lowest rate of use, and they also are the groups with the lowest levels of education and the poorest accessibility conditions.

The complex interrelationship between labour-force participation and fertility is suggested by the data. Clear patterns emerge, indicating that the productive role of women is affected by family-forming aspects, since having children and a spouse diminishes female participation. However, data suggest that the restriction of children on female work appears to be more strongly related to children's age than to their number. Similarly, the reproductive behaviour of women is negatively affected by labour-force participation: those with work experience bear fewer children than those who have never worked. Our data suggest that the increase in the cost of women's time as a consequence of their higher levels of education have led to higher female participation. All these interrelationships illustrated from a static cross-point of view are examined in a longitudinal and causal frame of reference in the next chapter, where we develop the multivariate analysis of the demographic transition processes of family formation.

4

WOMEN'S REPRODUCTIVE AND PRODUCTIVE BEHAVIOURS OVER THE LIFE-COURSE

The last section of chapter 3 provided a static view of women's demographic behaviour, and hinted at some interrelations with socio-economic characteristics. The present chapter provides a dynamic view of women's reproductive and productive behaviour. It depicts the timing, sequencing, and number of changes in discrete statuses characterizing the family formation process and women's productive behaviour over the life-course. Using longitudinal data, it also examines the determinants of occurrence of those single events (transitions between statuses) related to reproduction (first marriage, first birth, second birth, and third birth), and to production (entering into the labour force). Thus, the first section of this chapter considers reproductive behaviour as affected by women's status at the time each event occurs, while the second focuses on productive activities as affected, among other things, by women's previous reproductive history.

Women's Reproductive Behaviour: The Family Formation Process

By comparing the cohorts representing the behaviour before and after the demographic transition, we can identify changes, by socio-economic strata, in family formation processes, and examine women's status and other socio-economic factors associated with the occurrence of those processes.

Changes in the Family Formation Process

The complete histories of fertility and nuptiality allow us to identify and analyse changes in family formation processes. Coale's nuptiality model pattern was adjusted to observed nuptiality patterns to estimate the singulate mean age at first marriage for each cohort. This is especially important for the younger cohort, which is censored at a younger age. These models allow us to extrapolate the portion of the marriage pattern that is unobserved. Although the younger cohort may be too young to obtain reliable frequencies, it is still useful to obtain some idea of its likely behaviour.

To adjust the first marriage model standard frequencies to the actual experience of each cohort, it is necessary to select three parameters: C, the ultimate proportion ever married or in union; a_0, the earliest age at which first marriages can be observed; and k, the factor that relates the pace at which first marriages take place to the standard pace. For both urban and rural cohorts, the parameters were determined by a maximum likelihood procedure.

Figures 3 to 6 show the first marriage frequencies observed and adjusted for the younger and older urban and rural cohorts respectively. The ability of the model patterns to duplicate the observed patterns is clearly evident.

Tables 25 and 26 show the parameters a_0, k, C, and SMAM for the urban and rural cohorts, derived from the adjusted model patterns. Figures 7 to 10 show the frequencies at first marriage and the proportion ever in union, by age, from the adjusted models. The urban age at first marriage[1] is around 21.5 years and the proportion of women ever married is 91 per cent for both cohorts. For the rural women, the figures are 20.4 years and 87 per cent.

It is also clear from the table and graphs that there have been substantial changes in the family formation phase and that there are great differences between socio-economic strata. The urban upper stratum has experienced major changes in the family formation process. If we had not compared socio-economic strata, we would have erroneously concluded that no major changes in family formation had occurred.

However, behind the great similarities between urban cohorts at the aggregate level, there were large differences in behaviour by stratum. In the upper stratum there was no significant increase in the mean age at first marriage (from 22.1 to 22.6), but at each age the proportion of marriages declined, dropping from 85 to 62 per cent. Figures 8 and 10 clearly show marked changes for the urban upper stratum, but a fairly stable pattern in all rural and lower and middle urban strata. Similarly, a life table for the risk of first marriage constructed separately for strata confirms this conclusion. Table 27 presents the quantiles of the survival function to first marriage; that is, it shows the estimated ages at which 75, 50, and 25 per cent of the women are still single. There are clear differences in survival functions between urban and rural areas, but there are no clear differences between strata for the rural area. Thus, the data indicate, as did cross-sectional data analysed in the previous chapter, that the most important changes in marriage patterns have occurred among women in the urban upper stratum.

This differential behaviour is of great importance, since even in extreme cases where one would not expect any change in the marital fertility of upper-stratum urban women, a decline in their total fertility is observed. This is due to the fact that the observed total fertility pattern is the product of two patterns: the nuptial-

(Continued on page 56)

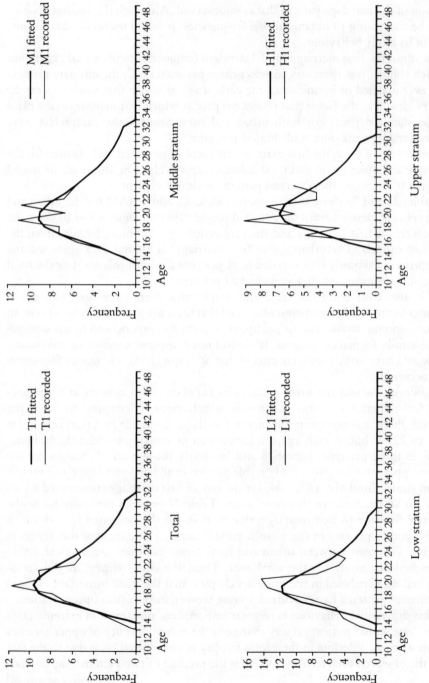

Fig. 3. First-marriage frequencies recorded and fitted by model schedule by socio-economic stratum, younger cohort, urban area

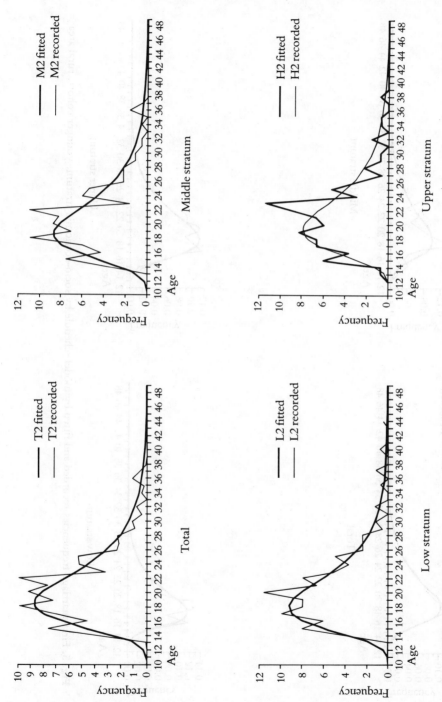

Fig. 4. First-marriage frequencies recorded and fitted by model schedule by socio-economic stratum, older cohort, urban area

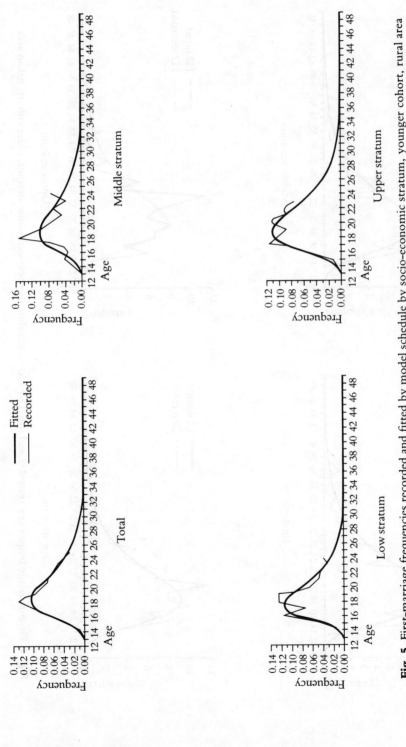

Fig. 5. First-marriage frequencies recorded and fitted by model schedule by socio-economic stratum, younger cohort, rural area

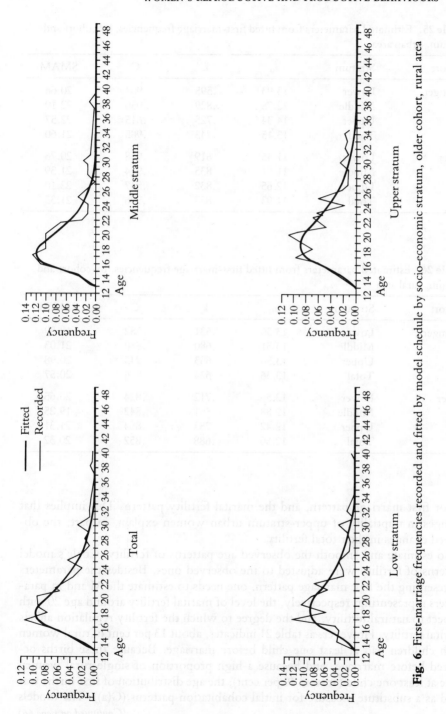

Fig. 6. First-marriage frequencies recorded and fitted by model schedule by socio-economic stratum, older cohort, rural area

Table 25. Estimated parameters from fitted first-marriage frequencies, by cohort and stratum, urban area

Cohort	Stratum	a_0	k	C	SMAM
Younger	Lower	13.93	.595	.904	20.68
	Middle	12.78	.829	.950	22.19
	Upper	14.34	.725	.615	22.57
	Total	13.15	.743	.905	21.60
Older	Lower	11.45	.819	.968	20.76
	Middle	11.91	.835	.924	21.39
	Upper	12.65	.832	.847	22.10
	Total	11.93	.827	.926	21.33

Table 26. Estimated parameters from fitted first-marriage frequencies, by cohort and stratum, rural area

Cohort	Stratum	a_0	k	C	SMAM
Younger	Lower	13.36	.531	.782	19.39
	Middle	13.31	.680	.880	21.03
	Upper	13.56	.653	.943	20.98
	Total	13.36	.634	.876	20.57
Older	Lower	12.56	.712	.824	20.65
	Middle	12.88	.561	.842	19.25
	Upper	12.42	.783	.884	21.31
	Total	12.50	.688	.852	20.32

ity or first marriage pattern, and the marital fertility pattern. This implies that changes in nuptiality of upper-stratum urban women explain, in part, the observed changes in their total fertility.

To estimate and smooth the observed age patterns of fertility, Coale's model patterns of fertility were adjusted to the observed ones. Besides the parameters representing the first marriage pattern, one needs to estimate the M and m parameters representing, respectively, the level of marital fertility around age 20 with respect to natural fertility, and the degree to which the fertility regulation affects marital fertility. However, as table 21 indicates, about 13 per cent of rural women with children had at least one child before marriage. Because these births occurred before marriage, and because a high proportion of single rural women have at least one child (around 40 per cent), the age distribution of first births was used as a substitute measure for initial cohabitation patterns (G(a)). The models

(*Continued on page 66*)

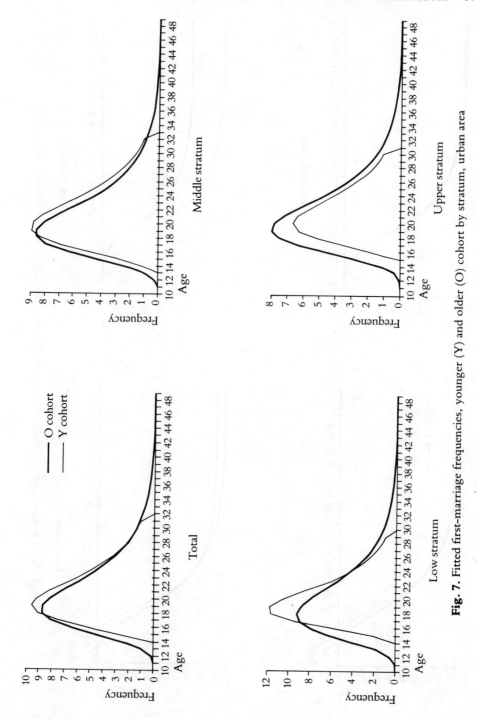

Fig. 7. Fitted first-marriage frequencies, younger (Y) and older (O) cohort by stratum, urban area

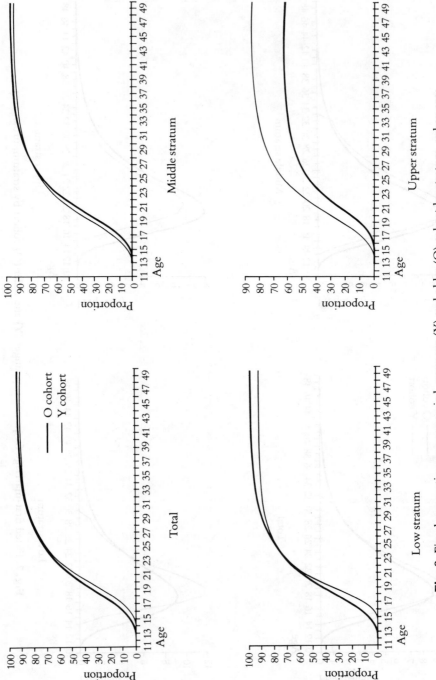

Fig. 8. Fitted proportions ever married, younger (Y) and older (O) cohort by stratum, urban area

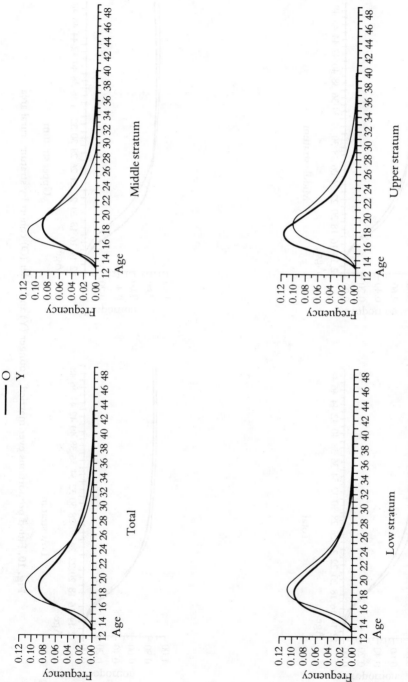

Fig. 9. Fitted first-marriage frequencies, younger (Y) and older (O) cohort by stratum, rural area

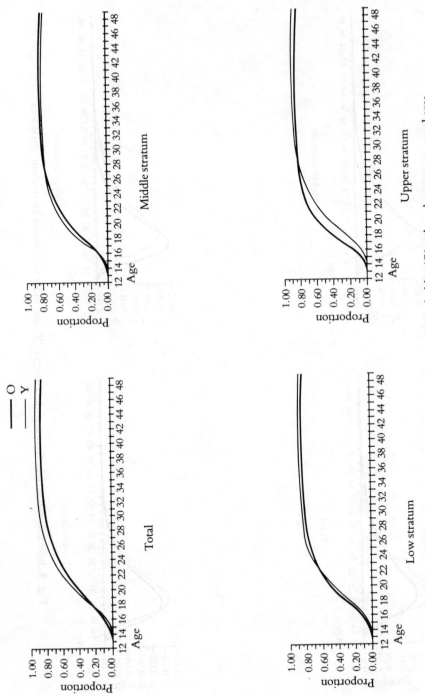

Fig. 10. Fitted proportions ever married, younger (Y) and older (O) cohort by stratum, rural area

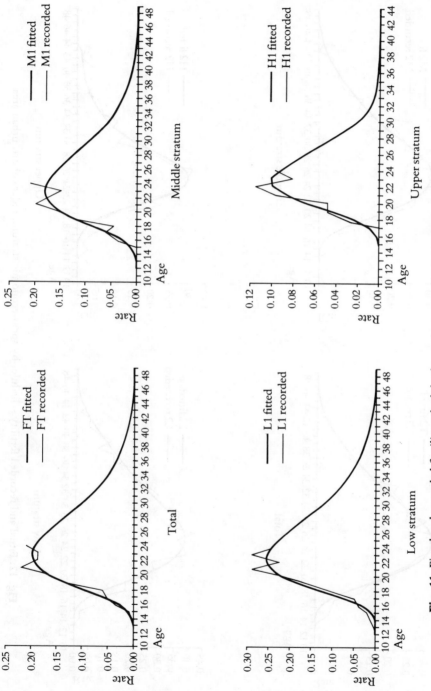

Fig. 11. Fitted and recorded fertility schedules by socio-economic stratum, younger cohort, urban area

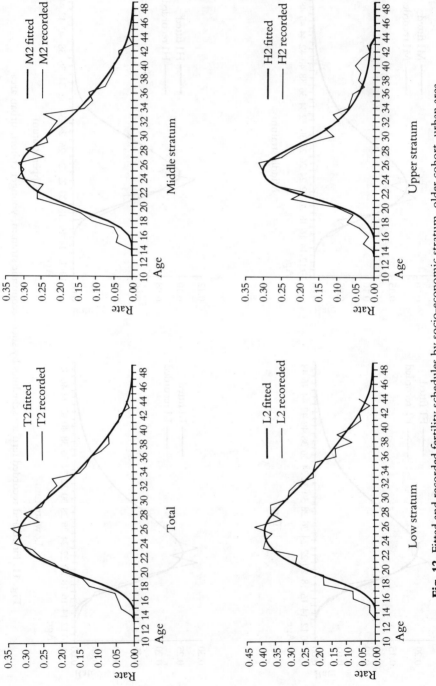

Fig. 12. Fitted and recorded fertility schedules by socio-economic stratum, older cohort, urban area

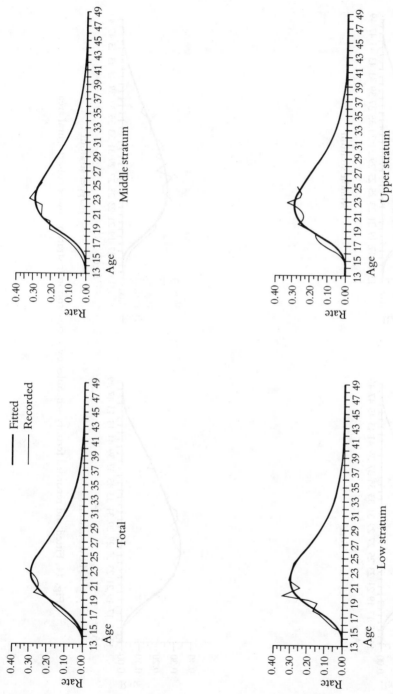

Fig. 13. Fitted and recorded fertility schedules by socio-economic stratum, younger cohort, rural area

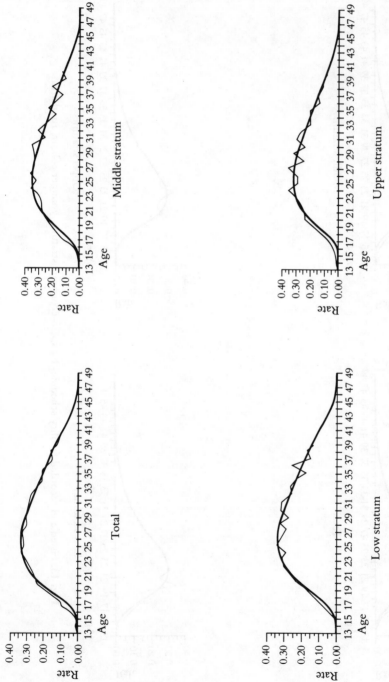

Fig. 14. Fitted and recorded fertility schedules by socio-economic stratum, older cohort, rural area

Table 27. Quantiles of the grouped survival function to first marriage

Group		Urban area			Rural area		
Cohort	Stratum	75th	50th	25th	75th	50th	25th
Younger	Lower	18	20	23	18	19	25
	Middle	19	22	—	18	20	25
	Upper	21	26	—	18	20	24
Older	Lower	17	20	24	18	20	26
	Middle	18	21	25	17	19	23
	Upper	19	22	27	17	20	25

Table 28. Estimated parameters from fitted fertility schedule, by cohort and stratum, urban area

Cohort	Stratum	M	m	TF[a]	a[b]
Younger	Lower	0.90	1.92	3.23	26.0
	Middle	0.75	2.11	2.36	26.0
	Upper	1.37	5.14	0.88	23.9
	Total	0.85	2.03	2.57	26.0
Older	Lower	1.44	1.14	4.96	28.0
	Middle	1.47	1.48	4.52	27.8
	Upper	2.58	3.10	3.23	26.7
	Total	1.45	1.42	4.70	27.9

a. TF = Total fertility rate.
b. a = Mean age of the fertility schedule.

Table 29. Estimated parameters from fitted fertility schedule, by cohort and stratum, rural area

Cohort	Stratum	M	m	TF[a]	a[b]
Younger	Lower	1.10	2.62	3.38	24.5
	Middle	1.16	2.13	3.56	25.5
	Upper	1.13	2.61	3.29	24.8
	Total	1.13	2.41	3.41	25.0
Older	Lower	1.09	0.59	6.03	29.0
	Middle	1.08	0.56	6.25	28.6
	Upper	1.17	0.71	5.60	28.7
	Total	1.11	0.63	5.97	28.7

a. TF = Total fertility rate.
b. a = Mean age of the fertility schedule.

were then adjusted by a maximum likelihood procedure. Figures 11 to 14 show the fertility patterns observed and adjusted for area and each cohort by stratum.

Tables 28 and 29 present the parameters related to the adjusted patterns. A sharp decline in both urban and rural fertility from the older to the younger cohorts, as well as an increase in the index of family-planning use, m, is evident. The total fertility rate decreased from 4.7 to 2.6 from the older to the younger urban cohorts, and from 6.0 to 3.4 for the rural cohorts. The family-planning index increased from 1.42 to 2.03 in the urban cohorts and from 0.63 to 2.41 in rural ones. However, although there is an increase in family planning in both areas in all strata, a greater decrease in total fertility is observed among urban women in the upper stratum.

Figures 15 and 16 show the changes from the older to the younger cohorts from the adjusted fertility schedules. The sharper decline in fertility of upper-stratum urban women could be due in part to the greater changes that they experience in their first marriage rates. By comparison, urban women in the middle and lower strata and all rural women decreased their total fertility rate without significant changes in nuptiality.

Life tables for birth intervals were also estimated, and summary results (quantiles) are presented in table 30. These indicate that for the younger urban cohort, the major changes in fertility behaviour have occurred in the inter-birth intervals (spacing between children), while the protogenesic interval (period between marriage and first child) has not changed substantially. This suggests that family planning has been used by the younger cohort mainly to space its children, and to achieve a smaller family size.

Rural data show that the small family size of the younger cohort is achieved with no major changes in the protogenesic or inter-birth intervals. This implies that fertility decrease from the older to the younger rural cohorts has occurred mainly as a consequence of the use of family planning after the desired family size has been obtained. This result is reinforced by ethnographic evidence of women's perceptions about family planning (chapter 5). Rural women, even those of the younger cohort, favour birth control "but among married women. . . once they have had some children."

In summary, urban and rural data suggest that although the mean age at first marriage has remained fairly constant across cohorts in both urban and rural areas (around 21.4 in urban and 20.4 in rural areas), the changes in the age pattern at first marriage for upper-stratum urban women have produced the most substantial fertility decline for this group. Nuptiality has not played an important role in the fertility decline of urban women in the low stratum, or all rural women. Rather, it has been mainly through the use of birth control that these women have achieved smaller families. However, there seems to be an important difference between urban and rural areas in the use of birth control. Urban women achieve smaller families by using contraception to space births, whereas rural women use planning only after they have obtained their smaller family size.

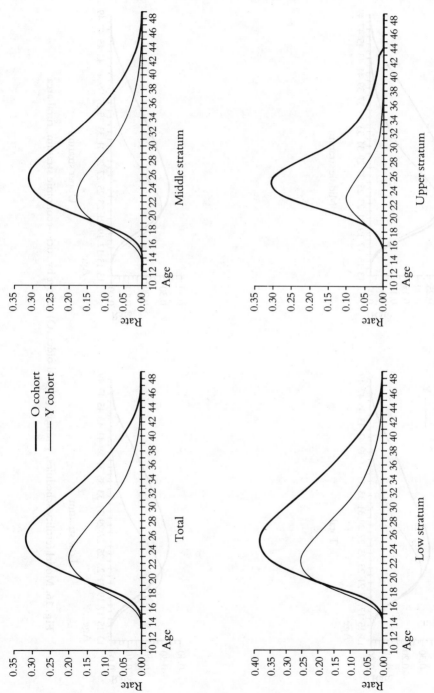

Fig. 15. Model fertility schedules, younger (Y) and older (O) cohort by socio-economic stratum, urban area

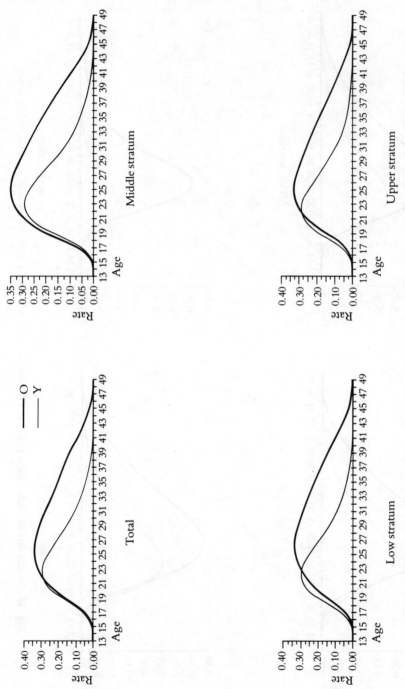

Fig. 16. Model fertility schedules, younger (Y) and older (O) cohort by socio-economic stratum, rural area

Table 30. Quantiles of the grouped survival function to selected parities, by interval, married women

Group		Urban			Rural area		
Cohort	Stratum	75th	50th	25th	75th	50th	25th
1. First parity (by duration since marriage)							
Younger	Lower	1	1	2	1	1	2
	Middle	1	1	2	1	1	2
	Upper	1	2	4	1	1	2
Older	Lower	1	1	3	1	1	3
	Middle	1	2	3	1	1	3
	Upper	1	2	4	1	2	3
2. Second parity (by duration since first birth)							
Younger	Lower	1	2	4	1	2	4
	Middle	2	4	6	1	2	3
	Upper	2	3	4	1	2	3
Older	Lower	1	2	3	1	2	3
	Middle	1	2	3	1	2	3
	Upper	1	2	3	1	2	3
3. Third parity (by duration since second birth)							
Younger	Lower	2	3	6	2	2	4
	Middle	2	6	8	2	2	4
	Upper	3	5	—	2	2	4
Older	Lower	1	2	3	2	2	3
	Middle	2	2	4	1	2	3
	Upper	1	2	5	1	2	3

Women's Status and the Family Formation Process

Having identified the changes in the family formation process, we turn now to its socio-economic correlates. Proportional hazards life-table models are used to examine the relationship between the rate of risk of occurrence of demographic events in the family formation process (first marriage and the first three parity progression ratio) and women's status when a given event occurs. This analysis utilized the complete life-histories on demographic as well as on socio-economic variables that define women's status.

According to the conceptual framework defined in chapter 2, origin and place of residence were included as socio-economic variables, and education and work activities were used to represent women's status in all the estimated models. Additionally, in models of parity progression ratios, demographic variables, such as use of family planning and age at the previous event, were included. All the socio-economic, demographic, and women's status variables were considered as categorical variables. With the exception of origin, they refer to (up to) the moment of occurrence of the event under analysis, or to (up to) the moment of the interview if the woman was censored with respect to that specific event. For example, in the case of the models for the hazard of first child (marriage), the variables refer to the moment of birth of the first child (marriage), or to the moment of the interview if the women has not yet had her first child (is still single) and is exposed to the risk of experiencing the event.

Five categories of education were considered: none, incomplete primary, complete primary, incomplete secondary, and complete secondary or more. Origin and place of residence were divided in the usual dual categories: urban and rural. Place of residence is used as a proxy to measure the effect of urbanization on the family formation process. Although it refers to the moment of occurrence of the event, previous estimated models considered, instead, years of residence in a city (urban centre). The fact that there was no statistically significant difference between the categories measuring length of time residing in an urban area (1 to 3 years and 4 years or more) led us to simplify the variable and use, instead, as we do here, place of residence.

Given the complex interrelationship between female work and fertility, two sets of categorical variables referring to work were included: work experience and work status at the moment of occurrence of the event. The first set was defined with the aim of examining the timing of the events. Work experience up to the moment of occurrence of events was considered to be an exogenous variable affecting the likelihood of occurrence of the specific events. It included four categories: none, experience in industrial activities, experience in services and commercial activities, and experience in agricultural and housework activities.[2] These categories were used to approximate the effect of type of activity (modern, transitional, and traditional) on the family formation process. The set of work-status variables refers to the year before the event occurred.

Although there could be a mutual causation between female work activity and the occurrence of the demographic event in the year of its occurrence,[3] we assume that work activity the year before avoids the bias that could otherwise be introduced. Work status is defined by the categories non-working, working in remunerative activity, and working in non-remunerative activity, with the aim of assessing the effect of occupational conditions on the process of family formation. All covariates were considered as non-time-dependent. Although a more complete analysis could be done by considering some covariates as time-dependent, the fact that we observe low occupational mobility among both urban and rural women, simple migration histories among rural women, and almost no entries into the educational system during the productive and reproductive span,[4] we decided, as a first approximation, to consider all covariates as non-time-dependent. Analyses of the data considering time-dependent covariates is a task for future research.

In order to check for the appropriateness of the use of the proportional hazards models, "stratified" models[5] were estimated for each set of covariates for each event under analysis (first marriage, first child, second child). Including all factors as covariates in the hazards models, and allowing the set of categorical variables to be tested to define the group, j, the corresponding baseline survivor functions estimates $(S_{0j}(t))$ were obtained,[6] and $-\log[-\log S_{0j}(t)]$ was plotted against time (or age) for each category of the variable (or group, j). Figures 17 and 18 show two examples. The functions were almost parallel for each case analysed, indicating that the assumption of proportionality was reasonable for each one of the considered sets of explanatory variables in each estimated model.

With the appropriate covariates, the partial likelihood procedure was used to estimate separate hazards models for each event under analysis, for each cohort and each socio-economic stratum within urban and rural areas. That is, in this set of models, we allow the baseline function *and* the set of coefficients to differ for all combinations of socio-economic stratum and cohort, producing twelve estimated models for each considered event. The hazard function at time (or age) t for an individual in the sth socio-economic stratum and the cth cohort is defined as:

$$h_{sc}(t; Z) = h_{0sc}(t) \exp(B' s_c Z)$$

where Z is the vector of covariates.

Comparison of the results within each area showed similarities across strata and across cohorts: all the socio-economic and women's status variables presented the same pattern of effects on the risk at each specific event, with only modest differences in their levels.[7] These results indicate no reason to estimate separate models for all six combinations of strata and cohort within each area. Evidence of changing patterns of family formation does not necessarily imply changes in the relationship between socio-economic and women's status explanatory variables and the family formation process.

Application of appropriate procedures and tests allowed us to simplify the estimated hazards models. Simplification of the models for each event under analysis was done in two steps. The first simplifying step was to collapse socio-economic strata within each cohort and each area. A "stratified" (grouped) model was estimated where *only* socio-economic stratum was allowed to define the groups with arbitrary and unrelated baseline survivor (or hazard) functions. Thus, in this set of models, the baseline function is allowed to differ for each socio-economic stratum and cohort, but the set of coefficients is constrained to be identical across socio-economic strata, but allowed to vary across cohort. The hazard function for an individual in the sth socio-economic stratum and c^{th} cohort is now defined as:

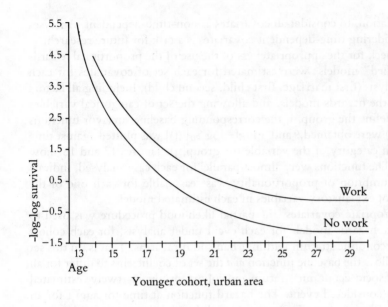

Younger cohort, urban area

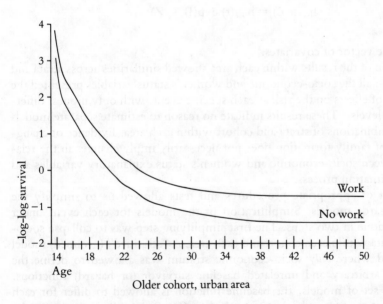

Older cohort, urban area

Fig. 17. Plot of −log (−log) of the survival to first marriage by work experience

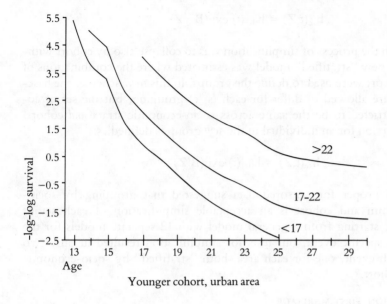

Younger cohort, urban area

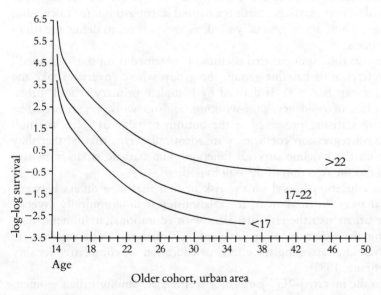

Older cohort, urban area

Fig. 18. Plot of −log (−log) of the survival to first pregnancy by age of first marriage

$$h_{sc}(t;Z) = h_{0sc}(t) \exp(B'_c Z)$$

The next step in the process of simplification was to collapse also by cohort within each area. A new "stratified" model was estimated where the combinations of stratum *and* cohort were used to define the groups. In this new scheme, the baseline functions are allowed to differ for each (s, c) grouping, but the set of coefficients is restricted to be the same across socio-economic strata *and* cohort. The hazard function for an individual in the sc[th] group is defined as:

$$h_{sc}(t;Z) = h_{0sc}(t) \exp(B'Z)$$

Statistical tests proper for censored data suggested that grouping by socio-economic stratum and cohort is an acceptable simplification of each set of models.[8] Thus, starting from a general model with 12 separate models for the hazard to each specific event, our tests for simplification resulted in only two models for each event, one for each area, both "stratified" by socio-economic stratum and cohort.[9]

FAMILY FORMATION: FIRST MARRIAGE

The focus here is the risk of occurrence of the event first marriage, that is, the risk of making a transition between single and married states. When estimating models for the hazard of first marriage, birth is a natural starting-point for calculating time of marriage. Thus, age is generally used, as we do here, to define the time-scale in such models.

Table 31 presents the exponentiated coefficients obtained from the "stratified" models. The reference or baseline group, the group where covariates take the value of zero (or exp $B'Z = 1$), is defined by complete primary school, urban origin, urban place of residence, non-working, and no work experience. The global chi-square statistic, presented at the bottom of table 31, tests the null hypothesis that all regression coefficients are identically zero, that is, that they have no effect on the baseline survival function. The statistic is far from significant, leading to the rejection of the null hypothesis.

The effect of educational level on the risk of first marriage differs between urban and rural areas. In rural areas, the relationship is monotonically inverse, whereas in the urban area the risk first rises with educational attainment, then falls, suggesting the existence of an inverted-"U" pattern. Both patterns are consistent with studies assessing the effects of education on cumulative fertility measures (Cochrane, 1983).

According to the inverted-"U" pattern, it seems that, among urban women, complete primary school is the point from which education begins to have a negative effect on the probability of getting married. Specifically, results indicate that, controlling for other variables, the hazard of first marriage for urban women with complete secondary or more education is about 60.4 per cent of the hazard

Table 31. Grouped proportional hazards models of first marriage by age

Variable	Urban area	Rural area
1. Educational level		
None	0.705[b]	1.235[a]
Incomplete primary	0.982	1.077
Complete primary	1.000	1.000
Incomplete secondary	0.750[b]	0.784[a]
Complete secondary or more	0.604[b]	0.529[b]
2. Work experience		
None	1.000	1.000
In industry	1.183[a]	1.034
In services	0.833	0.443[b]
In housework	0.729[b]	0.623[b]
In agriculture	N.A.	0.672[b]
3. Occupational status		
Non-working	1.000	1.000
Unpaid work	0.529[b]	1.174[b]
Paid work	0.631[b]	1.461[b]
4. Origin		
Urban	1.000	1.096
Rural	0.765[b]	1.000
5. Place of residence		1.356
Urban	1.000	1.000
Rural	1.578[b]	
Log likelihood	−4005.54	−4379.35
Global chi-square	148.96	69.06
d.f.	11	11
N	1074	1111
Generalized Wilcoxon chi-square	74.38	12.29
Savage chi-square	91.42	8.14
d.f.	5	5

a. $p < .05$ in two-tailed test.
b. $p < .01$ in two-tailed test.

for urban women of the same age with just primary school completed. Similarly, the hazard of first marriage for women with no education is 70.5 per cent of that for urban women with complete primary school (since $1/0.705 = 1.418$, we can say that the hazard for those with complete primary education is about 41.8 per cent greater than the hazard for those with no schooling).

The effects of educational attainment in rural areas, on the other hand, are very different. In this case, a peak hazard is found at the lowest level of education. The hazard of first marriage for rural women with no schooling is about 23.5 per cent greater than the hazard for those rural women with complete primary school, whereas it is 47 per cent ($= 1 - 0.529$) smaller than the hazard for those rural women with complete secondary or more education. This different pattern between urban and rural areas could be due to the still low educational attainment of rural women. As was mentioned earlier in this study, the average level of education for the younger rural cohort is 3.6 years (below complete primary) and 1.8 years for the older rural cohort.

Urban and rural results indicate that, with the exception of women who worked in industry before marriage, women with premarital work experience have a lower hazard of getting married at each age than women with no work experience. Although it has been observed in other studies that work experience in industry is related to modern occupations involving a high level of training, which usually have greater impact on women's aspirations and attitudes toward later age at marriage, the results we obtained might be an artefact of classifying tasks. For example, sewing done at home was classified as industry activities. When performed at home on a small scale, these activities have little to do with "modern" occupations, and do not require high levels of education. In this case, work experience in industry would not depress the risk of first marriage. If one collapses work experience in a dummy variable with only no or some work experience categories, the variable becomes highly significant, with this relationship obtaining in both areas: women who worked at all before marriage (or before the interview if censored with respect to the first marriage) have a lower risk of first marriage at each age than women with no premarital work experience.

Occupational status the year before the marriage is highly significant in both areas, although with opposite effects. The hazard of getting married for working urban women (independent of whether it is in paid or unpaid labour) is about half the hazard for non-working women. As we would expect, and as was suggested by the static cross-sectional analysis in the previous chapter, being engaged in work activities decreases the hazard of getting married. In rural areas, however, the hazard is greater for working than for non-working women, and is highest among those engaged in paid work. Although this is contrary to what one would expect, it is possible that in rural areas the contacts and social activities encouraged by work widen the female marriage market, increasing women's likelihood of getting married. This becomes more probable when we consider that paid work done by women in rural areas is mainly in the services sector (teachers, nurses, or even domestic employees), whereas non-paid work is mainly family agricultural work.

Urban and rural results show the same effect of origin on the risk of first marriage. In both cases, the risk of urban origin is higher than that of rural origin. It seems that the origin differentials sometimes observed in age at marriage could be due to differentials in educational attainment implicitly implied by place of origin. The educational opportunities open at the place of origin during one's youth determine the level of education individuals can obtain. Place of residence at the moment of occurrence of the event has consistent results in the urban study, but not in the rural. The hazard of first marriage for urban women who were living in a rural area is about 57.8 per cent greater than the hazard for urban women living in an urban area. The opposite is observed in the rural study. These unexpected results for the rural study could be explained, in part, by the small number of rural women with urban origin or with urban place of residence at the moment of occurrence of marriage. We must keep in mind that rural women are mainly of rural origin and almost half of them have not moved from their place of birth, while very few of those who have migrated to urban areas have returned to the rural area. If they have migrated to Bogotá, they are represented in the Bogotá urban sample as urban women of rural origin.

In summary, women's status variables, education, and work experience before marriage showed expected and significant effects on the hazards of first marriage, by age, in both urban and rural areas. Among the socio-economic variables, place of residence at the time of event exerts a non-trivial influence, whereas place of origin has no significant effect.

FAMILY EXPANSION

Since our concern here is with the reproductive behaviour of the family, the present discussion should be confined to married women and thus to marital fertility. However, as was mentioned before, a high proportion of single rural women have at least one child and some married women have had a birth before marriage. Table 32 presents the distribution of women by marital status (at the moment of the event or at the moment of interview if censored with respect to the specific event), by parity and cohort, for both urban and rural areas. Illegitimate births are more significant among rural women: 18.1 and 13.5 per cent of the younger and older cohorts, respectively, have had at least one illegitimate birth. In the urban area the figure is around 9 per cent for both cohorts.

The relatively high proportion of illegitimate first births, especially in the rural area, led us to an alternative definition of the population considered as exposed to the hazard of having the first child. Instead of being confined only to married women, we could consider all women as exposed to the risk of having a first child. However, this could distort the results, especially those related to use of family-planning methods. Since the data showed a strong relationship between use of family planning and marital status, and since the risk of childbearing is greater among married than among single women, we could observe in models including all women a positive influence of the use of family planning on the hazard of having the first child.[10] In the same way, the effect of other variables could be biased. For that reason, and since the sample size permitted, we conducted separate analyses of the risk of the first child for married and single women. For higher parities, not only did the proportion of illegitimate births diminish (see table 32), but the small number of cases did not permit the carrying

Table 32. Distribution of women at risk of reaching specific parity order, by marital status and parity order

At risk of first parity		Urban area		Rural area	
Marital status	Parity	Younger cohort	Older cohort	Younger cohort	Older cohort
Single	0	21.1	6.5	10.3	5.2
	1+	8.5	9.1	18.1	13.5
Married	0	4.9	1.1	2.0	1.2
	1+	65.6	83.3	69.9	80.1
(N=		578	496	533	578)
Second parity					
Single	1	4.4	1.1	4.1	1.1
	2+	1.9	4.8	5.7	8.7
Married	1	22.9	4.1	11.8	1.7
	2+	70.8	90.0	78.4	88.5
(N=		428	459	467	541)
Third parity					
Single	2	1.6	1.6	2.3	1.5
	3+	0.3	2.1	2.5	4.8
Married	2	48.6	10.3	23.2	4.6
	3+	49.5	86.0	72.0	89.2
(N=		311	435	393	526)

a. At moment of birth of child of specific parity or at moment of interview if censored with respect to the specific parity.

out of a separate analysis for single women. Therefore, for second and third parities, the hazards models were restricted to married women.

The hazard of having a first child for married women depends on age or, alternatively, time elapsed since the marriage. However, in the case of single women, the hazard depends only on age. For higher parities, models depending on age and duration since the previous event were estimated for married women. Socio-economic and women's status variables are the same as in the models for hazard of first marriage. In addition, two more categorical variables were included: use of family planning and age at previous event. Use of family planning was trichotomized as: none; use of modern methods; and use of traditional methods. As with other variables, use embraces time birth of the first child (or during inter-birth intervals for higher parities), or up to the time of the interview if the woman was censored (does not yet have the child of the specific parity).

Tables 33 to 39 present the urban and rural results from the different stratified

Table 33. Grouped proportional hazards models of having the first child, by age, married women

Variable	Urban area	Rural area
1. Educational level		
None	0.885	1.019
Incomplete primary	1.031	0.983
Complete primary	1.000	1.000
Incomplete secondary	0.910	0.784[a]
Complete secondary or more	0.769[a]	c
2. Work experience		
None	1.000	1.000
In industry	1.074	0.818
In services	0.852[a]	0.582[b]
In housework	0.960	0.854
In agriculture	N.A.	0.747[b]
3. Occupational status		
Non-working	1.000	1.000
Unpaid work	0.847	1.145[a]
Paid work	0.949	1.454[b]
4. Origin		
Urban	1.000	1.154
Rural	0.917	1.000
5. Place of residence		
Urban	1.000	1.191[a]
Rural	1.683[b]	1.000
6. Use of family planning		
None	1.000	1.000
Modern methods	0.875	1.103
Traditional methods	1.233[a]	1.082
7. Age at marriage		
At age 22 or before	1.000	1.000
After age 22	0.227[b]	0.163[b]
Log likelihood	−3108.28	−3218.45
Global chi-square	437.12	502.95
d.f.	14	14
N	821	852
Generalized Wilcoxon chi-square	45.50	18.40
Savage chi-square	51.20	25.50
d.f.	5	5

a. $p < .05$ in two-tailed test.
b. $p < .01$ in two-tailed test.
c. In the rural models, complete secondary and incomplete secondary or more were grouped into one category.

Table 34. Grouped proportional hazards models of having the first child, by duration since marriage

Variable	Urban area	Rural area
1. Educational level		
None	0.819	0.865
Incomplete primary	1.014	0.965
Complete primary	1.000	1.000
Incomplete secondary	1.004	0.925
Complete secondary or more	0.825[a]	c
2. Work experience		
None	1.000	1.000
In industry	1.051	1.087
In services	0.962	0.767
In housework	1.061	0.895
In agriculture	N.A.	0.851[a]
3. Occupational status		
Non-working	1.000	1.000
Unpaid work	0.924	1.067
Paid work	0.993	1.266[a]
4. Origin		
Urban	1.000	0.908
Rural	1.041	1.000
5. Place of residence		
Urban	1.000	1.229[a]
Rural	1.311[b]	1.000
6. Use of family planning		
None	1.000	1.000
Modern methods	0.985	0.764[a]
Traditional methods	1.169	1.059
7. Age at marriage		
At age 22 or before	1.000	1.000
After age 22	1.180[b]	1.048[b]
Log likelihood	−3400.36	−3623.14
Global chi–square	18.55	14.49
d.f.	14	14
N	821	852
Generalized Wilcoxon chi–square	33.40	18.56
Savage chi–square	38.50	22.52
d.f.	5	5

a. p < .05 in two–tailed test.
b. p < .01 in two–tailed test.
c. In the rural models, complete secondary and incomplete secondary or more were grouped into one category.

models for the hazard of having the first, the second, and the third child. The global chi-square distribution of each model, presented at the bottom of each table, indicates that, with the exception of the grouped urban and rural models for the hazard of having the first child by duration since first marriage and the rural model for the hazard of having the second child by inter-birth interval, all the estimated regression coefficients of all models are statistically different from zero.

Tables 33 and 34 present the urban and rural exponentiated coefficients for the hazard of having the first child, by age and duration since first marriage, for married women. The effect of educational level on the rate of risk of having the first child shows an inverted-"U" pattern in both models and in both areas. Again, the pattern indicates that having levels of education above the primary reduces the risk of having the first child in both urban and rural areas. Urban women with complete secondary education or more experience a risk 23.1 per cent (17.5 per cent) smaller than urban women of the same age (duration) with complete primary school. In the rural areas, an incomplete secondary education or more reduces the risk by 21.6 per cent (7.5 per cent) with respect to complete primary schooling. As mentioned previously, this inverted-"U" pattern has been observed in analysis of cumulative fertility measures in developing countries[11]; it was also suggested before in this volume in the cross-section analysis of chapter 3, where the most important differentials of fertility by education were observed above complete primary school.

In both urban and rural areas, work experience before the birth of the first child (or the survey, if censored) has significant negative effects on the hazard of having the first child. Specifically, work experience in services has the most significant effects. Urban women with work experience in services have a hazard by age of about 85.2 per cent of the hazard for those women with no work experience. For rural women the effect is even stronger, about 58.2 per cent. If one considers that industry could include some activities done at home, such as sewing, then "services" would be the category more similar to "modern" in the sense of distance from home, inflexibilities, and commitments, and would be the category with the highest opportunity cost of children.

Occupational status in the year prior to the occurrence of an event indicated that working urban women, independent of whether the job is paid or unpaid, have a lower hazard, by age and duration, of having their first child than non-working urban women. For the rural area, on the contrary, occupational status has a positive effect on the hazard by age as well as by duration. It is possible that rural women have no control over decision-making regarding fertility and, therefore, we could not observe a negative relationship between fertility and occupational activity the year prior to an event. This lack of control over decision-making among rural women is evident from the perceptions that women have of power relationships inside the household. The ethnographic work (chapter 5) shows that rural women are subordinated to their husbands. This fact, in turn, can be explained by the low levels of education among rural women. Similarly, since maternity determines the way in which rural women define their lives, the decision of having a first child may be independent of a woman's activity at that moment.

Urban as well as rural results show that, independent of the effects of other variables, origin does not influence the hazard of having the first child. Moreover, results of the models by age indicate effects opposite to those shown by the models by duration in both urban and rural areas. Place of residence shows more consistent results in the urban models than in the rural ones. Again, the unexpected rural result could be due to the small number of currently rural women having previously resided in an urban area. Currently urban women living in a rural area at first birth experience a hazard by age 68.3 per cent (or 31.1 per cent in the models by duration) larger than the hazard of those currently urban women who were already living in an urban area when the event occurred. This demonstrates the effect of factors related to the community of residence, such as presence of community contraceptive services, schooling and health services, and infrastructure in general, as well as economic opportunity costs.

Use of modern family-planning methods is usually negatively associated with fertility. Urban results for both models, by age and duration, indicate this negative relationship. In rural areas, however, only the model by duration did so. Urban women who have used modern methods of family planning have a hazard of having their first child of about 87.5 per cent (98.5 per cent) of that for urban women of the same age (duration) who have not used any methods at all. The use of traditional methods, on the contrary, rather than diminishing the hazard, increases it, perhaps because of the known high failure rates of traditional methods. This rural result largely can be explained by the attitude of rural women towards use of birth control. Rural women consistently oppose the use of family planning before having some children (see chapter 5). Thus, we could not expect a negative effect of regulation behaviour on the likelihood of having the first child, although it would be expected to affect the likelihood of having children of higher order parity.

The last variable included in the models as a control variable was age at marriage. Urban and rural results conform to expectations, indicating that later marriage decreases the hazard by age, whereas it increases the hazard by duration. Thus, urban (rural) women married after age 22 experience a hazard 77.3 per cent (83.7 per cent) smaller than the hazard of women who are of the same age but who married at age 22 or before. By contrast, urban (rural) women married after age 22 experience a hazard by duration since first married 18 per cent (4.8 per cent) larger than the hazard for those women of their same duration but married at age 22 or before.

Table 35 shows the exponentiated coefficients for the hazard models of single women having the first child. As in the case of the hazard models for first marriage, educational attainment has a different effect in urban and rural areas. In the

Table 35. Grouped proportional hazards models of having the first child, by age, single women

Variable	Urban area	Rural area
1. Educational level		
None	0.782	2.082[b]
Incomplete primary	0.764	1.195
Complete primary	1.000	1.000
Incomplete secondary	0.671	0.421[b]
Complete secondary or more	0.143[b]	c
2. Work experience		
None	1.000	1.000
In industry	3.679[b]	1.223
In services	1.320	0.913
In housework	3.655[b]	0.765
In agriculture	N.A.	1.048
3. Occupational status		
Non-working	1.000	1.000
Unpaid work	0.210[b]	0.760[a]
Paid work	0.534[b]	1.409
4. Origin		
Urban	1.000	1.050
Rural	0.798	1.000
5. Place of residence		
Urban	1.000	1.340
Rural	2.355[b]	1.000
6. Use of family planning		
None	1.000	1.000
Modern methods	3.810[b]	2.309[b]
Traditional methods	1.482	2.718[a]
Log likelihood	−292.51	−552.62
Global chi-square	66.53	54.15
d.f.	13	13
N	253	259
Generalized Wilcoxon chi-square	49.43	2.12
Savage chi-square	52.83	4.21
d.f.	5	5

a. $p < .05$ in two-tailed test.
b. $p < .01$ in two-tailed test.
c. In the rural models, complete secondary and incomplete secondary or more were grouped into one category.

urban area the relationship presents the inverted-"U" pattern, whereas in the rural area it is monotonically inverse. The effect of education on the hazard of having a first child is very strong and significant, especially in the rural area. Single rural women with no schooling have a hazard of having a first child 108.2 per cent larger than single rural women of the same age but with complete primary school. On the other hand, the hazard of a first birth among single rural women with incomplete secondary or more education is about 42.1 per cent of that for single rural women with complete primary school. This is what we would expect: uneducated single rural women are more likely to have a child.

Work experience and occupational status had strong and significant effects among single urban women. Having any previous work experience increased the likelihood of having a first child, especially if the work was in cottage industry or in housework activities (as domestics). This also is expected, since most single women in urban Colombia are domestics. Moreover, being occupied in any activity, paid or not, in the year of the occurrence of the event decreased the hazard by at least 47 per cent $(= 1 - 0.53)$.

Whereas origin has no significant effect on the likelihood of a first birth, the effect of place of residence is strong and significant among single urban women. Currently urban women living in rural areas have a hazard 135 per cent larger than the first-birth hazard of those women who are already living in an urban area at the moment the event occurs.

Use of family planning has a strong effect, but opposite to that expected. Use of modern and traditional methods increases the likelihood of a single woman having her first child in both urban and rural areas. This could be explained by two factors, which may act simultaneously. On one side, there could exist a correlation between use of family planning and exposure to the risk of having a child. That is, family-planning methods are used only by those single women having sexual relations, and hence with a high risk of having a child. On the other side, there may be high failure rates among single women principally because of lack of knowledge about the use of specific methods. This in turn could be a consequence of fear among single women of asking for birth-control information or services, since it is not socially acceptable for single women to use birth control, much less to admit openly that they have premarital sexual relations. This social rejection is evident from the analysis of women's perceptions of sexuality based on the ethnographic work (chapter 5). This hypothesis, however, needs further empirical verification, a task beyond the scope of this volume.

Tables 36 and 37 present the exponentiated coefficients for the hazards models of having the second child, by age and inter-birth interval. As mentioned earlier, these models are restricted only to married women. The effect of schooling on the hazards shows the inverted-"U" pattern in both urban and rural areas. Once again, the effect of education is negative only above levels of completed primary school.

The negative effect of work experience on the hazards by age is highly signif-

Table 36. Grouped proportional hazards models of having the second child, by age, married women

Variable	Urban area	Rural area
1. Educational level		
None	1.172	1.076
Incomplete primary	1.024	1.120
Complete primary	1.000	1.000
Incomplete secondary	0.722[b]	0.882
Complete secondary or more	0.558[b]	c
2. Work experience		
None	1.000	1.000
In industry	0.737[b]	1.014
In services	0.651[b]	0.690[b]
In housework	0.592[b]	0.718[b]
In agriculture	N.A.	0.749[b]
3. Occupational status		
Non-working	1.000	1.000
Unpaid work	1.193	1.089
Paid work	1.144	1.094
4. Origin		
Urban	1.000	0.944
Rural	0.907	1.000
5. Place of residence		
Urban	1.000	0.847
Rural	1.304[b]	1.000
6. Use of family planning		
None	1.000	1.000
Modern methods	0.836[a]	0.588[b]
Traditional methods	0.808[a]	0.938
7. Age at marriage		
Before age 20	3.685[b]	3.561[b]
At age 20 to 23	1.000	1.000
After age 23	0.252[b]	0.279[b]
Log likelihood	−2772.59	−3304.23
Global chi-square	647.89	663.27
d.f.	15	15
N	833	909
Generalized Wilcoxon chi-square	27.64	14.66
Savage chi-square	28.93	19.02
d.f.	5	5

a. $p < .05$ in two-tailed test.
b. $p < .01$ in two-tailed test.
c. In the rural models, complete secondary and incomplete secondary or more were grouped into one category.

Table 37. Grouped proportional hazards models of having the second child, by duration since first birth

Variable	Urban area	Rural area
1. Educational level		
None	1.050	0.987
Incomplete	1.082	1.062
Complete primary	1.000	1.000
Incomplete secondary	0.847	0.941
Complete secondary or more	0.734[a]	c
2. Work experience		
None	1.000	1.000
In industry	0.849[a]	1.127
In services	0.857	0.861
In housework	0.793	1.141
In agriculture	N.A.	1.008
3. Occupational status		
Non-working	1.000	1.000
Unpaid work	1.072	1.040
Paid work	1.045	0.948
4. Origin		
Urban	1.000	0.966
Rural	1.008	1.000
5. Place of residence		
Urban	1.000	0.788[b]
Rural	1.351[b]	1.000
6. Use of family planning		
None	1.000	1.000
Modern methods	0.801[b]	0.595[b]
Traditional methods	0.875	0.832
7. Age at marriage		
Before age 20	0.927	1.024
At age 20 to 23	1.000	1.000
After age 23	1.004	0.915
Log likelihood	−3068.37	−3683.86
Global chi-square	115.68	22.80
d.f.	15	15
N	833	909
Generalized Wilcoxon chi-square	70.46	6.05
Savage chi-square	50.05	4.07
d.f.	5	5

a. $p < .05$ in two-tailed test.
b. $p < .01$ in two-tailed test.
c. In the rural models, complete secondary and incomplete secondary or more were grouped into one category.

icant in both urban and rural areas, independent of the type of activity in which women engage. As can be expected at this parity level, the effects of work experience are stronger in urban than in rural areas, probably a consequence of the higher opportunity costs of children in urban areas. Occupational status the year the event occurred did not exert significant effects in either area. Thus, again, the relationship between work and the hazard function is determined not by the occupation at the year of occurrence of the event, but by work experience up to the moment the event occurred. It seems, then, that decision-making regarding fertility is a cumulative process over life, not affected by the kind of activity done once the decision has been taken.

Urban and rural results did not indicate any significant effect of origin, when controlling for other variables, on the hazard of having the second child, by age or inter-birth interval. Again, place of residence is the variable showing the effect of urbanization. Thus, for example, urban women who were living in a rural area have a hazard of having their second child 30.4 per cent greater than the hazard of those currently urban women already living in an urban area.

The higher the parity, the higher the effect of family planning on fertility. Use of family-planning methods, modern or traditional, have a significant negative effect on the hazard of having the second child, by age and by inter-birth interval. Thus, for example, rural women who used modern (traditional) methods during the preceding birth interval have a hazard of having their second child 40.5 per cent (16.8 per cent) smaller than the hazard of those women on the same birth interval who did not use family planning at all during the interval. Age at first birth was used here as a control variable and it showed the expected significance and results, especially for the models by inter-birth interval.

Tables 38 and 39 present the exponentiated coefficients from the hazards of having the third child, by age and inter-birth interval, for both urban and rural areas. Educational attainment has the inverted-"U" pattern effect in urban and rural areas, with higher levels of significance in the urban area. Complete primary school is the level above which increased schooling has a negative effect on the hazard rates. Urban women with complete secondary or more education have a hazard of having a third child 43 per cent smaller than the hazard of those urban women of the same age with complete primary school.

Work experience in any type of activity has a negative effect on the hazard rates by age and by previous inter-birth interval among urban women. The effect is not that clear for rural women. In the rural models the effect by age is negative only for work experience in services and agriculture. In the rural inter-birth interval models, work experience in agriculture has a negative effect, but it is very close to 1.0, suggesting no effect on the hazard rate. Thus, data suggest that for models on the likelihood of women entering a third parity order, work experience has negative and significant effects in urban areas, but not in rural areas. This suggests, as expected, greater incompatibility between the productive and reproductive roles among urban than among rural women. Occupational status in the

Table 38. Grouped proportional hazards models of having the third child, by age, married women

Variable	Urban area	Rural area
1. Educational level		
None	0.974	1.060
Incomplete primary	0.864	1.188[a]
Complete primary	1.000	1.000
Incomplete secondary	0.698[b]	1.096
Complete secondary or more	0.570[b]	c
2. Work experience		
None	1.000	1.000
In industry	0.951	1.082
In services	0.807[a]	0.834
In housework	0.683[b]	1.056
In agriculture	N.A.	0.821[a]
3. Occupational status		
Non-working	1.000	1.000
Unpaid work	1.187	1.170[a]
Paid work	0.964	1.693[b]
4. Origin		
Urban	1.000	0.892
Rural	1.024	1.000
5. Place of residence		
Urban	1.000	0.748[b]
Rural	1.213[b]	1.000
6. Use of family planning		
None	1.000	1.000
Modern methods	0.745[b]	0.295[b]
Traditional methods	0.771[a]	0.841
7. Age at marriage		
Before age 22	2.889[b]	4.552[b]
At age 22 to 25	1.000	1.000
After age 25	0.339[b]	0.200[b]
Log likelihood	−2025.10	−2876.82
Global chi-square	552.06	731.52
d.f.	15	15
N	724	867
Generalized Wilcoxon chi-square	26.50	5.21
Savage chi-square	29.58	7.67
d.f.	5	5

a. p < .05 in two-tailed test.
b. p < .01 in two-tailed test.
c. In the rural models, complete secondary and incomplete secondary or more were grouped into one category.

Table 39. Grouped proportional hazards models of having the child, by duration since second birth

Variable	Urban area	Rural area
1. Educational level		
None	0.982	1.063
Incomplete primary	0.951	1.116
Complete primary	1.000	1.000
Incomplete secondary	0.819[a]	1.031
Complete secondary or more	0.624[b]	c
2. Work experience		
None	1.000	1.000
In industry	0.982	1.076
In services	0.951	1.035
In housework	0.874	1.095
In agriculture	N.A.	0.967
3. Occupational status		
Non-working	1.000	1.000
Unpaid work	1.186	1.076
Paid work	1.004	1.253
4. Origin		
Urban	1.000	0.972
Rural	1.089	1.000
5. Place of residence		
Urban	1.000	0.862
Rural	1.245[b]	1.000
6. Use of family planning		
None	1.000	1.000
Modern methods	0.680[b]	0.268[b]
Traditional methods	0.677[b]	0.791[a]
7. Age at marriage		
Before age 22	0.958	1.090
At age 22 to 25	1.000	1.000
After age 25	0.758[b]	0.718[b]
Log likelihood	−2190.08	−3245.11
Global chi-square	189.36	71.70
d.f.	15	15
N	724	867
Generalized Wilcoxon chi-square	57.08	8.09
Savage chi-square	49.63	9.58
d.f.	5	5

a. p < .05 in two-tailed test.
b. p < .01 in two-tailed test.
c. In the rural models, complete secondary and incomplete secondary or more were grouped into one category.

year of occurrence of the event did not have clear effects in the models by inter-birth interval. In the models by age, results indicated that engaging in paid work negatively affects the hazard of having a third child among urban women, but the opposite was observed among rural women. Again, in the case of rural women, the importance of maternity and the lack of decision-making autonomy might explain the lack of a relationship between fertility and occupation at the moment of birth of children.

Origin and place of residence present the same effect that we observed for lower order birth. Origin has an insignificant effect, whereas place of residence has a strong and significant effect. By the birth of their third child, currently urban women living in a rural area have a hazard by age 21.3 per cent greater than the hazard of those currently urban women who were already living in an urban area.

The effects of contraception become more significant as the parity increases. Urban women who have used modern family-planning methods during the pre-ceding birth interval have a hazard of having their third child 25 per cent smaller than the hazard for urban women of the same age who did not use family plan-ning during the interval. For rural women the effect is even stronger, or about 70 per cent smaller $(= 1 - .295)$. Thus, it seems that use of family-planning methods is significant and similar for all parities among urban women, but grows stronger and more significant the higher the parity order among rural women. At stated before, this pattern is related to the position that rural women have on the use of family-planning methods; they favour birth control only after the woman has had some children. The control variable age at second child is significant in both models, by age and by inter-birth interval. Earlier age at marriage increases the likelihood of having a third child by age.

In summary, women's status variables, educational attainment, and work ex-perience have a consistent and significant effect on the likelihood of the occur-rence of transitions over the life-course characterizing the process of family ex-pansion. Education showed a consistent inverted "U"-shaped pattern, whereas work experience before each event showed a negative effect independent of the type of work activity. Among the socio-economic variables, place of residence played the most important role, showing the effect of higher access to schooling, health services, and contraceptive services in urban areas, as well as higher econo-mic and opportunity costs of female time. The use of modern family-planning methods showed significant and negative effects on the likelihood of all parity transitions among urban women. Among rural women, however, it was not significant for the first child, but its effect was significant for higher parities; the higher the effect the higher the parity. This result for rural women is consistent with their views on birth control, favouring its use only after the woman has had some children.

Women's Productive Work

The preceding section considered, among other variables, the effect of women's productive work on the reproductive behaviour of the family. That is, it considered transitions related to the family formation process as the dependent variable. Although that is the main focus of this study, we recognized that the relationship between women's work and fertility is complex – not unidirectional, but rather mutually dependent. Since the urban and rural longitudinal surveys provide women's occupational histories by cohort, we can examine the changes in the structure and pattern of female productive work as well as the socio-economic and demographic correlates of the likelihood of entering into the labour force. Thus, with the aim of contributing to the understanding of the complex relationships between women's work and fertility, the following analysis focuses on women's productive work and treats it as the dependent variable.

Patterns of Work

Labour-force participation refers to the proportion of the population, by age, in the labour market (employed and unemployed). Our life-histories data only allow us to compute patterns of employment defined as the proportion of the population of a given age that is employed.[12] Thus, by definition and depending on the unemployment rates, work rates are lower than labour-force participation rates. However, for the purposes of our analysis only, participation rates in productive activities and employment rates are used interchangeably.

It should be noted that the definition and classification of productive work used to construct the female patterns of work refer to the well-known definition and classification of the International Labour Office (ILO). This means that housework and plot work were excluded while family non-paid agricultural or non-agricultural work was included. Figures 19 and 20 present the estimated patterns of female work in urban and rural areas respectively. The great increase of female participation in productive activities from the older to the younger cohorts in both urban and rural areas is evident from the patterns. However, there are large differences in the level and shape of the patterns between urban and rural areas.

In spite of the fact that urban women of the lower and middle strata increase their participation, they reproduce the bimodal labour-force participation pattern of urban women in the older cohort in the same strata, at least up to the age they were at the time of the survey. This pattern reflects productive activity cycles and suggests incompatibility between the productive and reproductive roles of women. The younger urban women of the upper stratum, however, not only increased their participation in relation to the urban women of the older cohort in the same stratum, but, at least up to the survey date, did not reach a bimodal labour-force participation pattern. It seems that prolonged educational careers have postponed their labour-force participation at a level sufficiently noticeable,

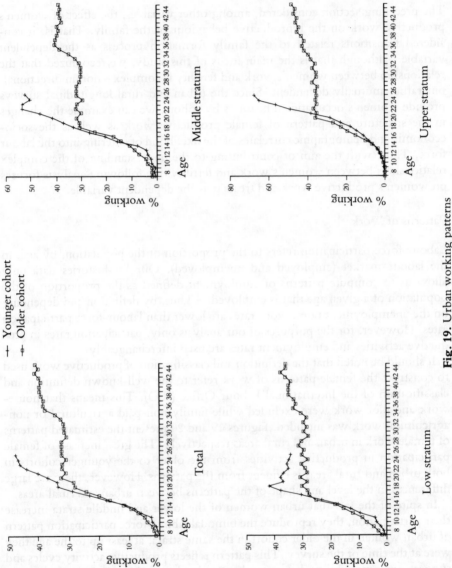

Fig. 19. Urban working patterns

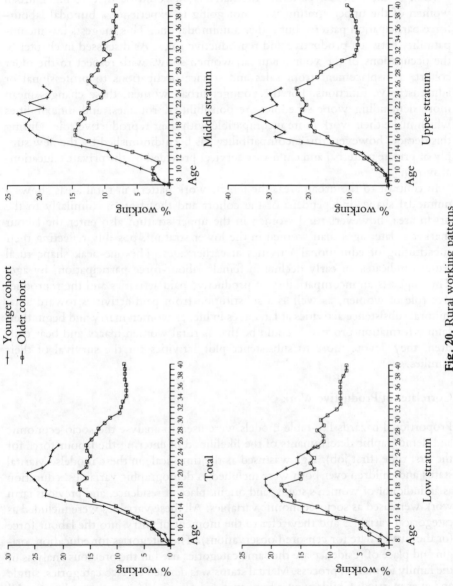

Fig. 20. Rural working patterns

so that at age 25, the age at which they censor, we did not observe the decreasing portion of the bimodal pattern. Alternatively, it could be that younger urban women of the upper stratum were not going to experience a bimodal labour-force participation pattern, but rather a unimodal one. This suggests less incompatibility between productive and reproductive roles. As discussed in chapter 3, the occupations of the younger urban women show, with respect to the older cohort, a displacement from sales and service occupations to professional or administrative functions. For the younger urban women, these changes mean more demanding work schedules, responsibilities, routines, and inflexibilities which make their work more incompatible with their reproductive role. During this decade, however, this incompatibility has been diminished by the new supply of private maternal and child-care services provided by the private educational system.

In contrast to the urban area, the female work pattern in rural areas shows a unimodal shape, independent of the cohort and the stratum. Similarly to the urban area, however, rural women in the upper stratum also enter the labour market at later ages than women in the lower stratum, possibly reflecting their substituting of educational activities at earlier ages. The one-peak shape rural pattern indicates an early decline in female labour-force participation, by age. This suggests an incompatibility of productive paid activities and the reproductive role of women, as well as a substitution from paid activities toward agricultural subsistence activities at later ages in life, as women marry and begin their family formation process. It could be that as rural women marry and bear children, they devote more to subsistence-plot activities for the survival of their families.

Correlates of Productive Work

Proportional hazards life-table models were used to analyse the socio-economic and demographic determinants of the likelihood of entering the labour force for the first time (first job). Age was used as the time-scale in these models. Marital status and children ever born were included as demographic variables, education as an indicator of women's status, and origin, place of residence, and previous farm work were used as socio-economic variables. All these variables were included as categorical variables and they refer to the moment of entry into the labour force (or the survey date for censored observations). The categories for education, origin and place of residence are the same categories used in the previous analysis of the family formation process. Marital status was defined by two categories: single and ever married. Children ever born was dichotomized into none and some. All covariates were considered as non-time-dependent as a first approximation to analysing the data. It is quite plausible that some variables, especially number of children ever born, were time-dependent.

Table 40 presents the exponentiated coefficients from the simplified ("stra-

Table 40. Grouped proportional hazards models of working the first time, by age

Variable	Urban area	Rural area
1. Educational level		
None	1.253	1.606[b]
Incomplete primary	1.543[b]	1.111
Complete primary	1.000	1.000
Incomplete secondary	0.609[b]	0.733[a]
Complete secondary or more	0.492[b]	0.611[a]
2. Marital status		
Single	0.515[b]	0.333[b]
Married	1.000	1.000
3. Children ever born		1.000
None	1.000	0.058[b]
One or more	0.088[b]	
4. Origin		
Urban	1.000	1.204
Rural	0.849[b]	1.000
5. Place of residence		
Urban	1.000	1.132
Rural	1.996[b]	1.000
6. Previous farm work		
None		1.000
Some		0.679[b]
Log likelihood	−3520.40	−1974.63
Global chi-square	720.84	979.50
d.f.	8	9
N	1074	1111
Generalized Wilcoxon chi-square	43.19	55.43
Savage chi-square	62.98	64.39
d.f.	5	5

a. p < .05 in two-tailed test.
b. p < 01 in two-tailed test.

tified") models for urban and rural areas.[13] The global chi-square statistic is far from significant; e indicates that all regression coefficients are statistically different from zero, that is, they have an effect on the baseline hazard function.

Education of women is well known to be strongly related to female labour-force participation; increased education is often suggested as one way to raise women's status and to promote their participation in the labour market. A typical "U"-shaped pattern of current female participation by education has been observed in most developing countries, where the most highly educated and least educated are most likely to work (United Nations, 1985).[14] Although our data suggest a solid association between education and the hazard of first entry into the labour force, the relationship is monotonically inverse; that is, women with the highest levels of education have a hazard of working for the first time that is below the hazard of those women with lower educational levels. This relationship obtains in both urban and rural areas. Since we are dealing with hazards of working the first time and not with current work, a plausible explanation for our results suggests substitution of activities at an early age: the least educated women drop out from school and start working early in life, whereas women with higher educational levels do not start working until they finish school. This was suggested by the female work patterns by age. Being in the educational system delays entrance into the labour force and thereby decreases the likelihood, by age, of working for the first time. If we examine current work, as we did in chapter 3, we observe a positive relationship between socio-economic strata, educational attainment, and female work.

The relationship between marital status and work is clearly marked in both urban and rural areas. The hazard of entering into the labour force for single urban (rural) women is about 51.5 per cent (33.3 per cent) of the hazard for ever-married urban (rural) women. Thus, controlling for other factors, including age, married women are more likely to start working for the first time than single women. This could be related to the fact that single women are the ones who stay longer in the educational system and, therefore, start working later in life than ever-married women.

Children ever born has a significant but weak negative effect. The hazard of first work for urban (rural) women with one or more children is about 8.8 per cent (5.8 per cent) of the hazard for urban (rural) women with no children. These results suggest an incompatibility of productive and reproductive roles: women with children are less likely to begin working than women with no children. If one were able to control for the age of the children, the negative effect would certainly get stronger.

Origin and place of residence were significant in the urban model but not in the rural one. The hazard of entering into the labour force for urban women with rural origin is about 85 per cent of the hazard for those currently urban women of urban origin. By contrast, the hazard for currently urban women living in a rural area is about 99.6 per cent larger than the hazard for currently urban women already living in an urban area. Thus, community of residence strongly affects the likelihood of first working by age.

Previous experience in subsistence farm work was also included in rural models. It is clear from the data that it has a significant and strong negative effect. The hazard by age of entering into the labour force for women with some experience in farm work is about 68 per cent of that for women with no experience at all. This is reasonable, since women who are or have been engaged in farm work are more likely to go on with such activities than to change to more formal occupations.

In summary, hazards models of entering into the labour force indicated that among all statuses, demographic and socio-economic variables included, marital status at the moment of occurrence of the event (or at the moment of the survey, if censored) had the most significant effect. Because we were not able to control for the age of the children, the effect of children ever born was of smaller magnitude, yet it was still significant.

Summary

A comparison of the process of family formation over the life-course between older and younger urban and rural cohorts (representing the behaviour before and after the demographic transition) indicates that there have been substantial changes in the family formation phase as well as in the expansion phase, with great differences between areas and between socio-economic strata. Urban women in the upper stratum have experienced the most dramatic changes in the family formation phase (first marriage), which, in turn, explains the greater changes observed in their total fertility. In contrast, middle and lower strata urban women and all rural women have not experienced significant changes in nuptiality, yet they have experienced a decrease in their total fertility rate. Thus, for urban women in the high socio-economic stratum, nuptiality has contributed to their fertility decline, whereas for urban women in the lower stratum and all rural women, nuptiality has not played an important role in fertility decline.

The pace at which urban cohorts expand their families over their life-course indicates that major changes have occurred in inter-birth intervals, while the protogenesic interval has not changed substantially. This suggests that family planning has been used by the younger urban cohort mainly to space children in order to obtain a smaller family size. Rural data indicates, on the other hand, that the small family size of the younger cohort is formed with no major changes in the protogenesic or inter-birth intervals. This demonstrates that family planning has been mainly used after the desired family size has been achieved. This result is supported by the qualitative findings on rural women's perceptions, which indicate that rural women favour birth control only after they have had some children. Thus, longitudinal data analysis, as well as qualitative information, suggest an important difference between urban and rural areas in the use of birth control in the process of forming their families.

The beginning and expansion phases of the family formation process are highly affected by women's status indicators at the time specific events occur: women's educational attainment and work experience. Urban and rural results indicated that educational level exerts an inverted "U"-shaped pattern effect. Completing elementary school is the point from which education begins to have a depressive effect on the likelihood of occurrence of various life-course transitions in the family formation process (first marriage and first parity progression ratios). If one relates this retrospectively to the life-course of urban and rural women, it is clear that the higher educational levels achieved by the younger urban cohort have largely been responsible for their higher changes in nuptiality and fertility. In spite of the observed increase in educational levels in all urban and rural strata, there remains a concentration of primary educational level in rural areas, of primary and secondary levels in the lower and middle urban strata, and of higher educational levels in the upper urban stratum. So, given the inverted-"U" relationship between education and the likelihood of successive transitions defining the family formation process, it is the urban women from the upper stratum who are relatively favoured by the increase in educational levels in terms of their changes in nuptiality and fertility.

Work experience showed a negative effect on the demographic transition processes of family formation, independent of the type of work activity, whereas occupational status in the year of occurrence of the event did not show a significant and consistent effect. It seems that the relationship between work and the hazards of family formation transitions is determined not by the type of activity, but by contact with the labour market. Experience in modern or traditional activities decreases the likelihood of the occurrence of the events in relation to non-worker women. However, the effect of work experience is stronger in urban than in rural areas, suggesting, as expected, a higher opportunity cost of children in urban areas. The non-significance of occupational status in the year of occurrence of events suggests that decision-making regarding fertility is a cumulative process over life, and is not affected by the kind of activity done once the decision has been taken.

Urban and rural results indicate that, independent of the effect of other variables, women's origin did not have a significant effect on the likelihood of occurrence of the different demographic events that characterize the process of family formation. It seems that the differentials by origin which are sometimes observed in cumulative fertility are due to differentials in education implied by the place of origin. Although origin had no major effect, place of residence at the moment of occurrence of the events showed an important effect. This evidences the influence of better access to educational, health, and contraceptive services, and to better infrastructure in general, as well as the higher economic and opportunity costs of female time in urban areas.

The use of family planning did show significant and negative effects on the likelihood of all parity transitions among urban women. Among rural women, however, it did not show a significant effect on the likelihood of reaching the first parity, but it did have significant and negative effects on the reaching of the second and third parities, the effect being greater the higher the parity.

An increase in female labour-force participation was observed simultaneously with the decrease in fertility from the younger to the older urban and rural cohorts. Higher levels of education usually increase the opportunity cost of women's time and lead to greater levels of participation. Thus, the higher educational attainments of the younger cohorts can explain, in part, their observed higher participation by age in productive activities. Data show that the younger cohorts stay in the educational system longer and postpone their participation in productive activities in comparison with older cohorts. This pattern reflects the fact that schooling has a monotonically inverse effect on the likelihood of entering the labour force.

The relationship between female productive and reproductive behaviours is not unidirectional but rather complex. As female labour-force participation has an effect on the likelihood of occurrence of the transition processes of family formation over the life-course, demographic characteristics related to the family formation process, such as marital status and children ever born, have effects on the likelihood of entering into the labour force. Marital status was the variable with the most significant and strongest impact on the hazard of working for the first time. Similarly, children ever born revealed the incompatibility of productive and reproductive roles among urban and rural women. However, the effect of fertility on the likelihood of entering into the labour force was diminished by our inability to control for the age of the children.

5

WOMEN'S PERCEPTIONS OF THEIR LIVES

As indicated before, the aim of the qualitative part of the study was to enrich and corroborate the longitudinal life-course results by analysing the changes between cohorts in the way women perceive their roles, their relations with their companion, their children, their community, and society in general. Although we considered aspects such as marriage, family size, sexuality, maternity, abortion, family planning, cohabitation, work, power relations within the family, and female participation in different social contexts, this chapter focuses only on those topics relevant in qualifying the observed women's reproductive and productive behaviours over the life-course.[1] The analyses use, as much as possible, the postulates of the ethnomethodological school.[2]

Construction of Analytical Categories

This section describes the process of systematizing the data and constructing analytic categories that facilitate the identification of patterns of meaning used by women in conceptualizing their lives. The construction of these analytic categories both aided in the understanding of the internal logic of each woman's statements and facilitated an aggregate analysis that sought patterns of meaning valid for the different groups of the sample, mainly by stratum and cohort.

The methodology designed by Patton (1980) was followed to identify the cultural patterns that permeated the points of view expressed by the women, taking into account the natural variations within the information as well. The interpretation of the data began from the cultural perspectives of those interviewed, according to the reflections on the themes proposed by the researchers. In the process of constructing the analytical categories derived from these pers-

This chapter was written by Elssy Bonilla.

pectives, a careful examination was made of the central elements identified in each response in order to locate the analytical patterns that guided the behaviour of the women as they expressed it. Emphasis was given to detecting the interpretative element used by women to reflect on themselves and their lives.

In constructing the analytical categories, two aspects derived from the Garfinkel conceptual framework of ethnomethodology (Cuff and Payne, 1985) were considered as determinants: on one hand the need to treat the features of the social setting as identical with the ways in which members perceive and recognize such features, and, on the other hand, the need to answer questions such as how members achieve such perceptions of their circumstances and how these perceptions inform their actions. In the process of manipulating the qualitative data the goal was to pass from empirical observation to the body of knowledge accounting for the observed activities, in order to understand the general cultural patterns at work. This was a process of continual feedback between the empirical and the conceptual levels.

Conceptualization of Women's Lives

The perceptions that women have of their lives are captured and summarized under the following major topics: sexuality, maternity, family planning, and power relationships. Although urban and rural women use similar categories to conceptualize their lives, the meaning and implications are not necessarily the same, as can be observed in the following analysis.

Sexuality

Sexuality has been considered by different studies as a central aspect of women's subordination.[3] Female sexuality in our culture takes on a more than strictly personal meaning from the moment at which part of man's dignity does not depend on his behaviour but on that of his companion and, accordingly, the honour of the family depends mainly on its women's prudence. The patterns of cultural knowledge concerning sexuality among the rural women clearly and consistently expressed a view of sexuality differentiated by sex. This conceptualization, which gives men wider scope and liberty in sexual behaviour while restricting the conduct of women in accordance with ethical and moral norms, is based on tradition and social custom, and does not necessarily reflect the individual's rational thoughts on the subject. In fact, the theme of sexuality traditionally has not been a topic of conscious reflection in rural Colombian communities, at least in the Andean area. As a consequence, established social practice becomes the point of reference and legitimates the appropriate sexual development of all group members.

A point of contrast was established when questions were asked about behaviours which run counter to traditional norms (e.g. premarital relations) but which clearly occur to some degree in the rural environment. This was evident from the life-history data, which indicated a high proportion of single rural women with children. Elements of change were also observed when inquiring about the necessity of educating young people about topics related to sexuality. Thus, an initial and tentative acceptance of the discussion of these issues was perceived in as much as women could reflect on their own lack of knowledge and on the implications that this lack of knowledge had for their lives. The specific themes discussed with the women were the meaning of sexual relations based exclusively on procreation and the acceptance of premarital relations.

SEXUAL RELATIONS BASED EXCLUSIVELY ON REPRODUCTION

Urban women in the younger cohort, independently of the stratum, said that sexual life was not limited to procreation. They pointed out that it was a right acquired by couples and that their companions shared this opinion. Sexuality and procreation are two realities that must be treated independently, without subordinating the first to the second. Among older women this division is not clear. Even though some of them think like the younger cohort, the majority consider that to separate sexuality from procreation "is to go against God's will"; but they point out that their husbands do not necessarily share this opinion.

Among the younger and older cohorts of rural women a clear difference on this matter was not observed. In general, the women interviewed were not in agreement with the idea that couples should only have sexual relations when they want to have children. Nevertheless, their subordination to the sexual demands of their husbands was manifested in expressions such as "one is under the command of the husband," "from the time you marry, you are under this obligation," and "when they want it, you have to give it to them." Sexually speaking, the wife should be available to "service" her husband without considering her own interests, which in turn highlights the virtual absence of expressed female pleasure in sexuality. In addition, these statements are affected by the double moral standard of sexual behaviour, which is explained with reference to the "different" nature of man and woman: "If you're a woman, yes [you would have sexual relations only to have children], men no," and "they need to use your body." When asked if men agreed with a solely procreative relation, a majority of the group said no. The difference in male power and male perceptions and female submission was reiterated. Some said that "they need a woman when they want it" and "they decide what to do."

SEXUAL PREMARITAL RELATIONS

Analysing this and the previous aspect together, a clear difference by cohort is detected among urban women in the way they conceived sexuality. Older women defined it from a clear moral perspective, considering sexual relations exclusively for legally married couples. This cohort does not agree with pre-marital sexual relations because it considers them to be morally improper. Exploring this aspect, it was possible to see what at first appearance was appraised as moral. Looking more deeply, we find that "moral" has some specific connotations that reveal how culture establishes clear differences between the sexes, placing women at a disadvantage to men.

Younger urban women approved sexual relations in single women, but their opinions differed by stratum. The upper and middle strata agreed with such relationships because they believed that women have the same rights as men, and it was a good way of getting to know each other before marriage. From this perspective, these young women appraise sexuality in a positive way, applying equal conditions to males. Younger women from the lower stratum did not identify themselves with equal sexual conditions. For them, premarital sexual relations were conditioned to the use of contraceptives, since they thought that in these situations they ran a high risk of being cheated by their companion and even of being rejected if they got pregnant.

In the rural area, two-thirds of the women manifested their disagreement with premarital sexual relations; the remaining third were located mostly in the middle and upper strata and among the older women. In rejecting premarital relations, although the ethical and moral dimensions were mentioned, two other analytic categories assumed importance: social sanctions and distrust of men's motives. On one side is fear of social sanctions, which are exerted particularly towards women; on the other is an element of distrust in men's sincerity, since men can "ridicule you," "toss you on the junk pile," or "trick" women with whom they have had relations without having made any formal agreement.

To an inquiry about the equal rights of men and women to engage in premarital relations, a large majority of women answered that this was not the case; this opinion was unanimous among younger rural women from the lower and middle strata. Few of the older rural women from the upper stratum claimed to support this idea of equality. In fact, they emphasized the double standard of sexual behaviour: "the woman should be more sensible," "a woman is faithful to one man only," "a woman should be careful and control herself." However, on the other side, men are considered "rovers" or "tom-cats" and "the man has a thousand times more freedom, they're not criticized." The older women who concurred on the possibility of equal rights for men and women in this matter suggested that the same rights should apply to both: "We should have this freedom because we are human beings equal to men. But for us, the women, we are branded for any little thing." "But we women have equal rights to those of men, it's just that unfortunately we have been denied this freedom to define our own lives, have our relationships. . . ."

The opinions of women on premarital sexual relations showed that among younger urban women of the upper stratum a greater change had occurred, since they also had an independent attitude to sexuality. Younger urban women from the lower stratum also accept premarital relations, but they do not trust their companions because they continue to accept a traditional view of the situation.

Maternity, Motherhood, and Women's Identity

Maternity determines women's lives because their lives have been defined by the capacity to be mothers, and this has placed them at the focal point of social reproduction. In this context, maternity has at least two meanings. On the one hand, it has become the basis of a cult that values women for their contribution as woman –mother, and, on the other, it suggests that "maternity" implies all the responsibilities inherent in the biological and social reproduction of children as well as the daily caretaking of husbands and other adult members of the household. Motherhood thus defined involves a contradiction: it is both an honour and a costly burden. On the altar of maternity women have sacrificed many aspects of their lives, accepting their exclusion from various social spheres and taking on a series of responsibilities with their husbands and children that should actually be shared with them and other social institutions.[4]

When urban women were asked if the principal mission of a woman was to assume her maternity, the reactions showed differences by cohort and stratum. Older women from all strata and younger women from the lower stratum approved of this statement, while younger women from the middle and upper strata had a different opinion. Older women commented that "women were born to be mothers," that it was "life's law," "the natural mission." They felt so sure that maternity was the principal role of women that they underlined this when talking about their own daughters, stressing that "they are women and their mission is to be ladies of the household and mothers," that this "is women's destiny," "the way a woman fulfils herself." Older women clearly expressed two dimensions on which they support and conceive their maternity. First, they said that children were a woman's reason for living. The way in which these women conceive the responsibility of maternity proves that they accept the rules of behaviour society has traditionally approved for the female population. Thus, maternity is a control instrument that exploits the concept of dignity. Women must "follow good behaviour" in order to deserve their children's respect. Each woman's child turns into the judge of her life.

Younger urban women from the lower stratum, like the older ones, said that maternity is the mission of women. They explained that their answer was based on religion: to be a mother is "to follow God's law" because "God made us women." This deterministic position towards maternity was also confirmed by their mothers' view that maternity should be the main responsibility of their daughters. Younger urban women from the upper and middle strata felt that even though maternity is important, it does not determine women's existence. For them, "women have other aims," "they can have children and do some other things at the same time," even "having children is part of life but it is not everything." Nevertheless, these younger women said, as did the others, that mothers are irreplaceable in the care of children.

The following aspects of the theme of maternity were discussed by the rural women: maternity as the definition of women's lives, and the importance of the mother for children. The idea of motherhood as woman's *raison d'être* is accepted by the majority of rural women without question, suggesting that it is an unavoidable responsibility for women and that their realization as persons depends on its accomplishment. A woman is incomplete and has not developed as a social being if she has not become a mother, because a central aspect of the logic of her life is to fulfil herself as such. This reality is joined to the fact that few women independent of the cohort think that, as a corollary, children are responsible for assisting their elderly parents, showing that for few women children are seen as a safety factor in a country in which the security of the elderly is quite uncertain. Even if a majority of the women see themselves as defined by their maternity, they also expect or hope that their children will pay them back in their old age when they can no longer support themselves. This idea is expressed by several of the younger women, such as one from the lower stratum who reflected that "to be a mother of a child is not only so that they can call you mom, but so that they also have to look after you later." Another young woman from the upper stratum indicated that maternity was the principal mission because "when you get to a certain age, you need someone to lean on, someone to help you."

Despite the fact that these comments reflect the majority view, it is true that most of the women felt they could assume the responsibilities of motherhood and also continue to fulfil themselves in other ways. Some define maternity as only one aspect of their female experience, but not the only one. A woman ought to undertake it as an important part of her life, but it should not totally determine her life, since, as a person, she is also capable of excelling in other areas.

Almost all rural women said that they were irreplaceable as mothers, in the sense of providing physical care and affection for their children. They strongly criticize women who do not undertake this task fully and without reserve. More than one-half condemned those women who were able to breast-feed and did not do so; some of them gave priority to the interests of the children over those of the mothers. These opinions are quite similar across cohorts and strata. Nevertheless, opinions on maternity have to be seen in the context of these women's lives; what becomes clear is that their expressed "traditional" views are blended with some recognition of change. For example, women did not reject the employment of women with young children outside the home. This was expressed not only in the abstract, as an opinion, but also when voicing their ideas and hopes for their daughters. An older woman from the upper stratum pointed out: "Today there's a lot of encouragement for women to work . . . one has to leave the children with someone to take care of them in order to work. You can't just stay around here . . . depending on your situation, when you get a chance to work you should do it . . . in this way we can help our husbands."

Younger rural women from the middle and low strata were the ones who expressed most clearly the possibility of simultaneously caring for children and taking on paid work. On the one hand, they think that a woman can decide for herself whether she should work, and, on the other, they ask themselves whether realistically they have the option of *not* working, given that their husbands' salaries are insufficient to cover necessities and that government support of their basic needs is very limited. This shows the beginning of a social critique of the value given to motherhood, as observed in the following comments by younger women of the lower strata: "I think that to work [for a wage] has become a necessity, and definitely you have to get someone else to look after the children . . . in any event you have to have a little time for them, even if it's only 5 or 10 minutes"; or: "With the salary my husband gets and the amount he contributes to the household, I don't have any alternative other than to earn a few cents . . . we would be even poorer." The contrast between the abstract definition of motherhood for women and the concrete situations in which they must undertake this role presents a real contradiction between ideology and praxis. Those who continue to give a determinant place and value to their role as mothers do so in a thoroughly uncritical and overly general fashion ("it's nice," "it's the best," "it's destiny").

Abortion

One of the most difficult aspects to analyse is the way women view abortion. The experience documented in various studies shows that women have an opinion about abortion that does not correspond to their specific experience. Studies done among women hospitalized for an abortion indicate that in spite of their situation they reject this practice (Sanz de Santamaría, in press). Similarly, data from the life-histories indicate that urban women from all strata have had abortions, and yet are against it.

All urban women disapprove of abortion, though some differences are observed by cohort and stratum in the way they explain their attitude. Older women from all strata and younger women from the lower stratum said that abortion was a sin because "it was to take a life," "to deny the right to be born" or "to act against a human being unable to defend himself." Younger women from the upper and middle strata said that "it cannot be asserted that abortion is a sin," "it depends on one's values," and "it is not a sin if you do it in time." These same women are the ones who say that abortion is not a crime because "sometimes it is necessary" and "you have to take into account the causes that led to the abortion, such as rape, economic necessity, and if she wants the baby or not." These younger women did not share the moral position of the older ones, but when the situation was analysed from their daughters' position, they said that they would prefer to try to understand them, giving advice about family planning and, if it is necessary, "they will help to bring up the child."

Abortion is a very contradictory aspect of women's lives. On one side there is the moral stance taken by the church, and the similarly negative position of the state against the practice. On the other side, society presents an open standard based on the promotion of an apparent freedom of conduct for women. These contradictions suggest that, in spite of "sexual freedom," a woman finds it very difficult to carry on a pregnancy if she is not legally married. Thus, a woman who has had an abortion faces a conflict, and it is probable that it is assumed with a high emotional cost. The nature of the social norms applied to woman – which determine that her sexuality and her dignity shall be in conflict – means that she must be ready to sacrifice her emotional balance to maintain her dignity as a person.

Among rural women, the condemnation of abortion on religious, ethical, and legal grounds is the general tendency. Some of the women from the upper stratum temper this general rejection and condemnation by analysing the characteristics of certain situations that women have to face. The strong religious and cultural tradition of rural Colombia, which has created an image of women destined for motherhood, sets up an ideological barrier that impedes any real reflection on the issue. For that reason, the rejection of abortion assumes importance, since abortion not only signifies the denial of life to a new being, but also the absolute rejection of the mother's role.

Family Planning

Among urban women, the position on family planning varies more by stratum than by cohort. In fact, although all of them said that contraceptive use should not be an exclusively female practice, women from the upper and middle strata said that the decision to use them should be taken by the couple, and they pointed out that their companions approved of this use. They believed that contraception can be openly discussed by the couple. Women from the lower stratum said that they cannot discuss this in the same way because their companions are against the use of contraceptives. When they make the decision, they must hide it from the man, because he considers that to be his decision and that women should not offer opinions about it. Men from this stratum are against contraceptive use for two reasons. On the one hand, they do not have adequate information, so they wish to prevent the woman from planning her family; on the other hand, they think it can be harmful to her. Men from the lower stratum said that they lose control of a woman's sexuality if she uses family planning.

In relation to contraceptive use, a clear difference by stratum was perceived. While for upper and middle strata women the decision is generally taken by the couple, women from the lower stratum have to take it secretly because their companion disapproves. Younger women perceived their relationship with males in a highly subordinated way.

Among rural women, the majority of whom accept their ability to regulate family size, the use of measures to prevent conception is clearly understood. However, in their opinion the use of contraceptives should be strictly limited to married women. Their use by single women has a different connotation and implies loss of social status. An increased awareness of the social and individual costs of child-rearing can be observed, and the particular interest of women in birth control is highlighted as women come to recognize the physical and psychological effort that is involved in this process. Given the role that family planning can play in the observed process of reduction of family size in rural areas, a careful analysis of knowledge and opinions on the subject will be presented.

The acceptance of contraceptive use is a general tendency observed among rural women; only a few of the women from the middle stratum, most of them older, disagreed with the use of family-planning methods. The majority recognized the benefits of planning since "it is adequate," "it helps you avoid having a flock of kids." These benefits are justified in the light of the practical aspects of the regulation of procreation. Reservations about the use of contraceptives stem from two basic considerations: religious pronouncements that induce a non-reflective progression of the norm, and fear of health hazards. Women with the first type of reservation say, "better not to plan, because when children come the hand of God is in it," or "all because of the will of God." The second concern, health problems, shows a fear of the possible consequences of their use. An older woman from the middle stratum says: "I don't agree, because they say that contraceptives have many side effects, illnesses for women."

Although data indicate that the majority of rural women make joint decisions with their partners about the use of contraceptives, analysis of the content of some of the answers shows that it is simple. On the one hand, the comments indicate that women are afraid to make independent decisions that can result in retaliative actions by their spouse. In this sense, one older woman from the lower stratum said: "If it is only the wife, there are problems in the home, because the husband is going to say that if it is so she can have other relations . . . So I think in this sense that there ought to be a common agreement so that there won't be any . . . difference in the home." On the other hand, other rural women pointed out that the decision on the use of contraceptives was a matter for women because "the woman suffers, the man isn't interested in the number of children," "they don't see past having the children," "the woman gets pregnant and they don't do their part." In this sense, they make a moral judgment about male behaviour that reveals the irresponsibility and lack of interest of men in the situation of pregnant women and in the problems of rearing a large family. However, the exclusive use of family-planning techniques by women was strongly questioned independently of their cohort, showing once again a criticism of men's lack of interest and responsibility in matters related to the control of reproduction and its implications.

Rural women were asked for their opinions on the use of birth control by other women: first, their own daughters; second, their single daughters; and, finally, single women in general. The profile of answers given to the question referring to their preferences for their daughters is mixed, showing positive replies, negative replies, and conditional answers. More than half thought that their daughters could use contraceptive techniques, while the other group answered that it would depend on the specific situation of the daughter. In all strata, this agreement was associated above all with a pragmatic approach in which they affirmed that it is not always convenient, nor economically feasible, to have a large family. One younger woman from the upper stratum agreed: "Yes, surely, I would advise my daughter that when she marries the best thing is to plan to have only one child, and then, with ample time for planning, to have another, and that she should be thinking of the children she will have and know how she's going to educate them." Conditional responses encompass a more traditional view of the woman in the family. They suggest that the daughter can plan if she has already had several children and only if she is married. As a younger woman said: "When married, well yes. But after she has already had her children, yes."

The use of birth control by single daughters is rejected by the great majority of women of both cohorts. The main impression is that of great fear of the negative repercussions of such use in their later lives, such that they have "too much freedom," have "become corrupted," or have "problems with their future husbands." It could also affect their future possibilities of "getting a husband" and could unleash gossip in the community. Some of these opinions represent an extreme that identifies this practice as immoral and insane.

The use of contraceptives by single women in general is a controversial topic among rural women, with opinions both pro and con. The greater disapproval of this practice is found among women from the lower strata, half of whom disapproved of it, while one-third of the rural women from the middle and upper strata agreed with them. On the other side, approval of this behaviour comes primarily from upper-stratum women, half of whom accept the possibility, along with one third of the middle stratum and a very few from the lower stratum. Disapproval of the use of contraceptives by single women is linked with reflections of an ethical and moral nature that both reveal and support the existence of a traditional female behaviour pattern in rural areas. There is considerable suspicion of sexual relations that occur outside of the context of marriage, which can lead to "excessive licentiousness" or "adulterous vice"; a single woman "can sleep with a married man without caring about it." Statements like, "you shouldn't give in to a man, nor do those things before marriage," "it's a bad act," and "it shouldn't be that way" illustrate this rejection.

Power Relationships

One of the aspects most clearly associated with female subordination is women's location in the power hierarchy, in which they have limited possibilities for taking independent initiatives in important areas of their lives and which places them totally or partially, according to the characteristics of the person, under male jurisdiction. This in turn is a determinant in the socialization and protection of, and vigilance over, female behaviour, given the patriarchal character of Colombian culture and society.[5] This subjection is intimately related to the form in which women have been morally and economically dependent on men and to the way in which their social participation has been mediated by and through males. Woman's integration into the private domestic world has not only kept her at the margins of public life in many ways, but has also meant that in the accepted order of things she comes in second place behind her male companion.

Female dependency within the home has two dimensions that are not mutually exclusive. On the one hand, society gives men the moral and cultural attributes that allow them to control, judge, and sanction the behaviour of spouses and to delimit the space within which they can act more freely, and outside which they will be sanctioned. On the other hand, the behaviour of the sexes is regulated by a double standard that implies that a man can do what he wants because he is a man, as some interviewed women said, but a woman cannot because she is a woman. Thus men are given both the right to control the behaviour of women – who "ought" to comply with what men determine to be best for women and for the household, and to sacrifice their own interests as persons – and the exclusive right to her sexuality without the necessity of complying with the same norm. The household has been organized around patterns of obedience and loyalty that are differentially valid and differentially sanctioned according to sex.

The profound changes that have occurred in Colombian society during the period of demographic transition are intimately related to the fact that the female population has achieved educational levels similar to those attained by males and that women have also significantly increased their participation in the labour force. These changes have meant that the contribution of women to the reproduction of the household has had to be redefined and reanalysed in view of the greater complexity of their roles. This fact will undoubtedly transform the basis of family organization and the exercise of power within the household. Is the young cohort participating on an equal basis in the structure of power?

In the analysis of the authority line inside the household, urban women considered two aspects: the obedience that women owe to men, as well as the household decision-making process in relation to housing, education of children, family relations, and so on. Older women from the lower and middle strata saw their marital relations in terms of obedience, which implies that they restrict their conduct explicitly according to the man's will. They said that they must obey their husband because "if we don't obey him we are not doing anything," because "he is the husband and we have to obey him in everything," because "we see ourselves under their command," because "it is a natural law," because "if a husband treats you well, he will be interested in the best for me." This aspect is central to understanding the answers of these two groups to the question of who makes decisions. Women feel that it is a shared process and that both decide about the previous aspects just mentioned. However, analysing the way in which they explained the decision-making process, it is evident that "shared" doesn't mean that both are equal: "I consult him and obey what he decides" because "men are the responsible ones," because "they are the head of the household, but of course not alone and the decision is made as a group."

When rural women were asked whether "once married a woman ought to obey her husband," none from the upper stratum were in agreement on absolute obedience; they proposed that it was necessary to reach an agreement and make decisions that respect the views of both partners. This way of viewing relations with the spouse can be clearly seen in this observation: "One should only accept what is useful, because each spouse has his or her way of thinking and one doesn't have to obey if it is bad; there should be an agreement." In this group a more critical consciousness has developed around the issue, which is reflected in the thought of an older woman from the upper stratum who says: "There was a time before when you had to live subjected to your husband, to what he said, because you didn't control even one peso, you didn't have any rights and lived too much under his thumb, but now it's not that way. Now I have seen that life is better than that, that women have the right to speak out when they want to, because men too are also more educated." The importance that women give to the education of the husband in relation to his behaviour inside the home is clearly stated by a young woman from the upper stratum, who says: "I don't think that a man who mistreats a woman is an educated person, but a person who has no dignity, nor education, nor anything else, if he believes that he has the right to beat and mistreat the woman who married him."

Rural women from the older cohorts take a defensive position that has different connotations: "you don't have to let him humiliate you," "don't let him beat you to impose his will." This position in no way suggests that they think they are able to question the traditional norm. On the contrary, they assert that "I have always had this obligation to obey, although there are things that are unjust," "you have to let them dominate because you don't know how to defend yourself." In the acceptance of the husband's authority two interconnected dimensions can be found that allow a glimpse into this tradition: on one side a non-reflective acceptance such as: "it's your inheritance because Eve had to obey Adam," "the law gives the wife to the husband and if she doesn't obey he leaves," or "what he orders turns out well." On the other side, it is possible to detect a very pragmatic attitude that it is better to obey "because with that idea you avoid problems," or "you live better and avoid problems." Thus, when considering spousal relationships among rural women, differences by strata are more clearly visible than differences by cohort. Women in the upper strata are those who question this vertical line of male authority.

Talking about how children should be raised, all the urban and rural women said that this responsibility must be shared in a united decision. Nevertheless, they think that the father should educate the boys and mothers the girls, taking into account that "men are more difficult, women more obedient," "women are more delicate, men resist more," "women understand better," and "man has to be treated harder." In other words, in the process of bringing up children, although this is assumed by the couple, a different conception of personalities by sex is reproduced, reinforcing the idea of the "weakness" of women and "strength" of men.

Among urban women, the group in which more gender equality is perceived in relation to the household power relation corresponds to women of the upper stratum independently of the cohort. For them, women do not owe obedience to men because "both have rights and obligations," "both have to be submitted to the same things," "they have to share everything." In the decision-making process there is joint participation, and this fact must be understood not only from the perspective we have just discussed, but in relation to the way their children are educated. They do it together, emphasizing that girls and boys must be educated in the same way because "both are the same."

In summary, the analysis of power relations inside the household in the urban area shows differences by cohort and stratum. Older women from the middle and upper strata accept an inferior position and they pass this on to their children. Women from the upper stratum do not accept the subjection of a woman to her husband, and as a consequence they bring up boys and girls as equals. In the rural area, on the contrary, systematic differences between cohorts were not found. Although notions about power relations differed according to the perspective adopted, all the rural women displayed an acceptance of male power.

Work and Time Allocation

One of the most controversial topics in the study of the female population is how to conceptualize and measure women's work. The convention is to identify work with those activities for which a wage is received. The analysis of work done in the previous chapter indicated that this conception of work underestimates the participation of rural women in productive activities. This section presents the perception women have of their domestic and remunerated work. Closely related to this is the division of labour inside the household.

Perception of Work

An understanding of the way the urban woman tackles her work, and the degree of involvement of her mate, combined to raise a discussion about the female definition of household activities, the way in which their spouses perceive such activities, and the way women appraise their work vis-à-vis the perceptions of their spouse. An analysis of urban women's reactions to these different perspectives of work shows that, independent of the cohort and the stratum, women put as high a value on their domestic work as their productive activity, but they accepted the sexual division of these tasks. They consider that the household, and specifically the children, must be attended to by them, and they cannot be absolved from this duty "because the kids will suffer a lot"; therefore, the house is the responsibility of the mother even if she has to work outside the home or help the husband to earn the family income.

Urban women with few exceptions said that their activity is indeed work, because "one gets tired and exhausted" or "it is quite heavy." They have obligations that must be carried out, "but because we do not receive a salary it is said that it is not work." Urban women defined their domestic activity as work, but have not yet solved the contradiction inherent in the fact that they are primarily responsible for the household and yet help the husband if it is necessary to generate income. However, men have not become real helpers in the household in spite of the women's increasing work outside the home. Urban women from both cohorts value, on a conceptual level, their domestic work, but in real life they do not question the implied power relation in their double responsibility – paid labour and domestic labour. In fact, their double day would be lightened if the husbands participated in domestic tasks.

Women allocated their remunerated work depending on the way they conceived relations inside and outside the household. Even for the younger women, who claimed to have a superior degree of equality with the husband, maternal responsibility imposed restrictions on their personal life, independent of their ability in other matters. The male's absence from domestic work is reinforced by women, because even though they consider their remunerated work as important as the male's, they said that they wouldn't advise their daughters to work while they have small children, thus restricting female life to maternal responsibilities. This ambiguous position of urban women with respect to work can be understood better in the light of their daily experience in time allocation, to be analysed later.

With the aim of better locating rural women in the context of their experience, they were asked to enumerate all the activities in which they had invested their time during the year prior to the study. All rural women, with the exception of one, had participated in domestic work, most of which was combined with other remunerated activities. A sizeable group had undertaken more than one paid activity in addition to domestic work, especially in the cases of women from the lower and middle strata.

The importance given to reproductive activities appears in the fact that the great majority considered their principal activity to be domestic work, regardless of the number or intensity of remunerated activities they had undertaken. About one-quarter of the respondents, among whom the older women predominated, perceived their domestic activities as work because they are heavy and consume a significant part of their time and energy. The perception that some women have of their domestic work suggests that they have thought critically and systemati-

cally about this topic. Their perceptions are quite clear on the following major points:
1. Domestic work is exhausting and laborious because "women don't stop all day long," "women work like slaves every day with very little help from members of the family," and "it is very heavy work although men say that it's not work."
2. Domestic work is a thankless task because it's invisible, while the work that men do is more recognized. "Domestic work isn't seen, although other kinds of work are." "Work is only considered to be what men do."
3. Domestic work is unpaid "although if you do it in somebody else's house they pay you for it." Other comments along this line included: "it's not worth five cents," "nobody pays for it," "it is not lucrative." One woman even said that "I would like them to pay me for it because since it is not remunerated it makes me dependent."
4. Housework consists of multiple activities while "men do one thing at a time." It is intensive because it includes not only work in the household but also other responsibilities such as "taking care of the animals."

Those who expressed their understanding of the meaning of domestic work with the most clarity belonged to the upper stratum. Within this group, all the older women, when comparing their work with their spouses, reached the conclusion that women worked harder and more intensively than men. This will be corroborated later on in the analysis of the couples' use of time. According to what women said, women's work is heavier because it is continuous and because women are responsible for everything. This means that women run "from one side to the other without stopping, always busy and always rushing." Men, on the other hand, are less pressured because "they leave, they do their jobs, and they can relax on the weekends."

Those who seemed to be suffering most from their heavy workloads were women with fewer economic resources who said that poverty made their situation more difficult, especially when there was very little money, because this meant that they had to take on extra work. Although the majority of the rural women have begun to analyse their situation with respect to domestic work, they do not yet have a clear notion of how to confront the established division of labour, and they tend to accept it somewhat passively: "Although this work is unbelievably heavy and you don't get anything out of it, one has to have patience."

The reason for this resignation was clearly stated by a young woman from the low stratum, who said that despite everything "one has to eat and I don't have any choice." Women's lack of resolve in confronting this situation contains an element of self-defence that shows the insecurity of some of the women faced with a spouse whom they do not fully trust. This means that some women from the lower and middle strata accept the established order in terms that are quite non-reflective and subordinated, but that allow them not to assume a double labour load. "If the woman works [for a salary], the man becomes irresponsible"; "the woman does her job in the home and the man will look after getting what's needed for the shopping." Ambiguity is noted among the young women from the lower stratum who accept this division of labour by sex, indicating a profound uncertainty about this social division: "they are responsible for the woman and should make her respect him"; "if the woman goes out to work, she leaves the home and the housework." The nature of these quotations shows the complexity of women's perceptions of the "ideal woman." In fact, almost all the women engaged in some kind of income-generating activity. However, they continued to accept the social division of labour in the domestic sphere with its corresponding roles.

Use of Time

For the urban area, time budgeting during one day of the week as well as during the weekend were analysed by cohort, stratum, and family characteristics. The information was obtained from ten close observations, where the time allocation of the spouse was also observed. The daily working period was limited to women who spent part of the day at home, many of them doing domestic and remunerated work, so the ones doing all their remunerated work outside the house were excluded, because it was very difficult to interview them.

Time allocation in the urban area presents the following characteristics:
1. In the middle and lower strata, women who live with a mate have a longer working day than their companions. Usually they get up half an hour earlier, get breakfast ready for the family, and in some cases they also go to bed later at night.
2. Women that perform domestic work and remunerated work in their households assume this responsibility in a parallel way, without clearly identifying the domestic and productive time. This fact implies more exhausting working periods, and demonstrates that much of the remunerated work is seen as marginal by the women – in spite of this activity they defined themselves as housewives.
3. Younger women seem to organize the domestic work more efficiently. Their working periods are as long as those of older women, but though the majority have small children even they are receiving an income. It is evident that older women from the middle and lower strata are more confined to the house than the other women. There are various ways of accounting for this situation. These strata may possibly have a technical infrastructure support to domestic work less adequate than that of the upper stratum. Besides, the location of the lower-stratum households in the poorest areas of the city implies an inadequate access to public services, which means that in some of them there is no

running water, the energy service is deficient, and the cooking is done with gasoline or a similar kind of fuel, which is not only dangerous but consumes additional time.

4. The way families allocate time during the weekend shows that the working women concentrate a significant part of their domestic work on these days. However, it was found that their working periods are shorter and that they had some leisure time. Figures 21 and 22 illustrate the time allocation of two selected urban women.

One important aspect of the analysis of time allocation in the urban area is related to the activities individuals participated in. This perspective is especially needed when the female population is studied and even more when women assume domestic and remunerated work. Taking into account the way different members of the household participate in remunerated activities and in domestic tasks in urban areas, we found that every urban woman with a remunerated activity also did domestic work with no help from her companion, but women from the upper stratum engaged a domestic servant to ease the burden.[6]

The analysis of rural women's use of time was developed by obtaining information on all the activities carried out in the course of a week, not only on one weekday and one weekend day, as in the urban areas. A full week would cover the majority of rural women's productive and domestic activities. Even though some tasks must be done daily (cooking, child care, tidying, etc), others are undertaken less frequently (weeding, marketing, washing, ironing), owing to the nature of rural activities. We took into account both unremunerated domestic activities and productive activities, whether remunerated or not, and included the activities of both husband and wife. This part of the analysis refers to the organization of the household as a working unit within which tasks are allocated.

The main rural results indicate that the importance of domestic activities for the survival of the family and in the overall configuration of the lives of women can be better understood by considering the core of activities which constitute domestic labour. The data indicated that the majority of the women had direct responsibility for domestic work, a few were only helpers in the home, and only one woman, a single mother who lived with her parents and worked outside the home, did not do household work. The analysis showed that time use varied somewhat by cohort. All the younger women were responsible for domestic work, with the exception of two, who did not live with a spouse; one was a family helper and the other did not participate. In the case of the older women, not all were responsible for domestic duties. The separated women from this group, like the younger women mentioned above, did not have the primary responsibility for domestic labour. These worked as helpers, except for those who had no daughters. Figures 23 and 24 illustrate two examples of time allocation among rural women.

According to these data, domestic work determines much more in the lives of younger women, not only because they have young children who demand more

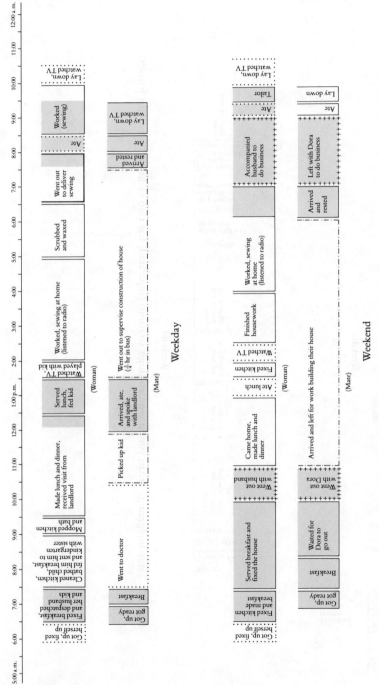

Fig. 21. Time budgeting, urban old women (middle stratum) (has five children, one two years old; husband is ill, doesn't work).

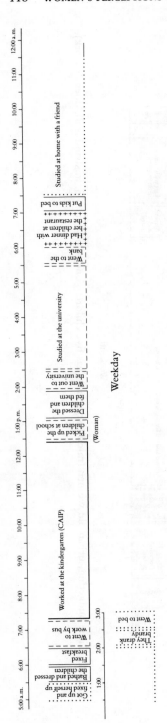

Weekday

Weekend

Fig. 22. Time budgeting, urban young women (high stratum) (separated, has two children, lives with friends).

attention but also because the children have not reached the age where they can assume these tasks. The participation of spouses in domestic work varied significantly by cohort. It was found that although the responsibilities assumed by men were quite similar across cohorts (bringing fuel, carrying water, marketing), there were many more young men who helped in these activities than older men. It may be that the children of older couples who have reached a certain age assume the domestic labour not only of the housewife but also of the husband. It is also possible, however, that what is being observed is a change in the contribution of men to household work. One younger man cares for the children and another takes charge of lunch on the day that the wife does the shopping, tasks that men traditionally do not do.

Using a strict definition of housewife – women engaged only in reproductive and unremunerated activities – only three women in the rural subsample could be so classified. All the rest carried out an income-generating activity and more than half took on two or three activities that earned an income for themselves or for their families. Of the latter, only one was not the person with primary responsibility for domestic labour as well. The work in which these women engaged was fundamentally agricultural (such as cultivating a family garden or bringing grass to feed the animals), but others had small businesses such as broom-making, knitting, and sewing, while another group tended the family store or acted as intermediaries in the sale of coffee and cattle. Finally, some received a salary for domestic work done in other homes. Thus, the range of activities undertaken is quite wide, although the majority of productive activities occur in the context of the home. Husbands worked in only one remunerated activity, with the exception of four who cultivated their land and also had another job.

Rural women were found to work very intensively. The combination of domestic and productive work that was evident in the time-budget analysis shows that they utilize their labour in the accomplishment of very different tasks within the same time period. The characteristics of the productive work that women do, the largest amount of which is carried out in the vicinity of the home, does not lead to the realization of a schedule of productive work, domestic work, and leisure. On the contrary, their use of time is somewhat arbitrary and depends on the requirements of the family for their services. In all cases in which women do both domestic and productive work, the responsibilities of the first determine the allocation of their time. The only exceptions are those women who work outside the home. For some, productive work is subjected to the requirements of reproductive work, even when their economic contribution is a determining part of the family income.

The husbands of the rural women also work long hours in paid work, and this includes work on Saturdays. However, given the marginal participation of men in domestic work and the characteristics of their work, for them the allocation of time to productive and to reproductive activities is not a problem in any way.

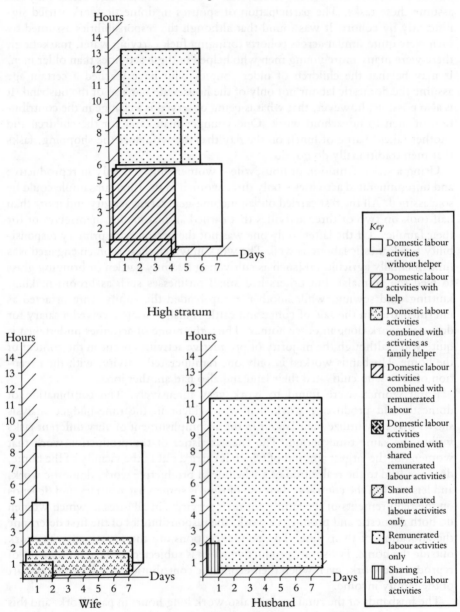

Fig. 23. Time budgeting, rural young women

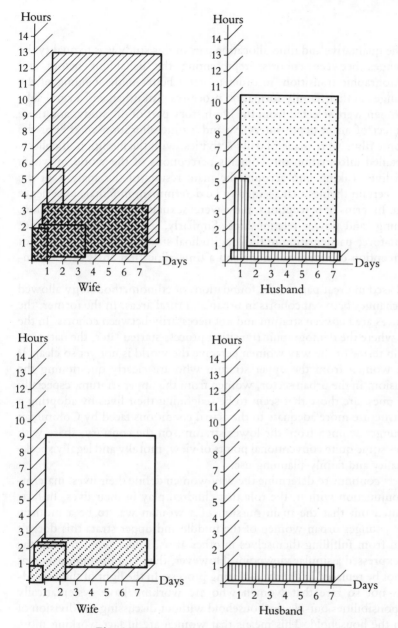

Fig. 24. Time budgeting, rural old women (low stratum)

Summary

The aim of the qualitative and time-allocation part of this study was to qualify the inherent changes between cohorts, representing the behaviour before and after the demographic transition, in order to get a better understanding of the observed changes in their family formation processes. An urban and a rural sub-sample of women were selected from the life-history part of the study, and these were the subject of an in-depth interview and a time-allocation chart. For the rural case, some films were made of daily activities, with the intention of collecting more detailed information on women's perceptions of the world in which they act and live. Taking into account the main results of the analysis of the life-histories, certain themes that seemed to be determinant in female experience were selected. In terms of perceptions, these were: sexuality, maternity, abortion, family planning, and power relationships. Similarly, given the importance of female labour-force participation in the longitudinal study, a detailed analysis of women's perception of work was done and a time-allocation analysis was conducted.

Analyses based in great part on the foundations of ethnomethodology allowed us to detect changes between cohorts in urban and rural areas. In the former, the main differences are between stratum and not necessarily between cohorts. In the rural sector, where the demographic transition process started later, the nature of the changes in terms of the way women perceive the world is not yet so clear. It seems to be women from the upper stratum who are clearly questioning the traditional vision. In the urban sector, women from the upper stratum, especially the younger ones, are those that seem to be redefining their lives by adopting a conceptual structure more adequate to the actual conditions faced by Colombian woman. Younger women from the lower stratum, on the contrary, share with the older ones some quite conventional points of view, morally and legally speaking, on sexuality and family-planning use.

Two aspects continue to determine the way women define their lives: maternity and, in conjunction with it, the role that children play in their lives. In fact, they all pointed out that the main mission of a woman was to be a mother, although for younger urban women of the middle and upper strata this doesn't prevent them from fulfilling themselves in other areas. Older women from the rural sector expressed a similar viewpoint. However, they said unanimously that women cannot be replaced in the child-rearing process. In the light of this consideration, it is not so rare that women who are working have systematically assumed responsibilities outside the household without discussing the division of work within the household. This means that women are in fact working more hours daily than their companions, who only participate in the domestic work, if at all, in a very marginal way. Thus, nearly all women have longer working periods than their companions and their intensity of time use is greater, given that every day they perform various activities at the same time. It can be expected that, in the future, the changes in women's conceptualization and perception of their lives will be reflected in a true reorganization and redistribution of domestic work.

6

CONCLUSIONS AND IMPLICATIONS

General Conclusions

Population trends in Colombia indicate that the demographic transition experienced by the country since the end of the 1930s has occurred with a lag of almost a decade in rural areas compared to urban areas, with large differences among socio-economic groups. The process occurred fastest in those sectors favoured with better socio-economic conditions.

The comparison of cohorts representing behaviour before and after the demographic transition in Colombia indicates that the transition has occurred through different changes in urban and rural areas and among socio-economic strata in the process of family formation, as well as in the attitudes toward variables affecting this process. In Bogotá, a metropolitan urban centre, there have been substantial changes in the formation and expansion phases, with great differences between socio-economic strata. Yet in comparable rural sectors, areas of Boyacá and Cundinamarca states located in the higher zones, there have been substantial changes in the expansion phase but not in the formation phase, with no major differences by socio-economic strata.

For urban women in the upper stratum, nuptiality changes have contributed to fertility decline; for those in the low and middle strata and all rural women, however, nuptiality has not played an important role in fertility decline. Urban and rural women in all strata have obtained their smaller family size through the use of birth control. However, there seems to be an important difference in the use of birth control between urban and rural areas. Urban women use it to space births in the process of obtaining a smaller family size. Rural women, on the contrary, use family planning once they have obtained a smaller family size. This could be related, among other things, to the perception rural women have about the use of family-planning methods. They agree that married women should control their family size, but only once they have had some children.

The development process experienced by the country involved changes in many interrelated aspects of life, such as health, education, female labour-force participation, urban–rural residence and the status of women. All these changes affected fertility. The characteristics of urban and rural women indicated that although there have been substantial changes in female educational attainments and labour-force participation in both urban and rural areas, low levels of education are still observed among rural women. Their low educational attainment is mainly due to the inability of the educational system to hold the population at primary levels, and to the limited access to secondary and higher levels of education.

Education in most circumstances reduces fertility. Urban and rural results show evidence that the lowering effect does not appear until higher levels of education are reached. Some primary education, in fact, appears to increase rather than decrease fertility. Apparently completed primary school is the level from which education lowers the probability of occurrence of the demographic events defining the family formation process (nuptiality and fertility). The increase in educational levels from the older to the younger cohort provided urban and rural women, especially rural women, with practical knowledge and with access to information along with a generally broader perspective. Contraception became more readily available, which led to the increase in birth-control use and the reduction in fertility observed in the country.

Female labour-force participation depends on educational attainment and is tied to place of residence. Higher levels of education increase the opportunity cost of a woman's time and lead to greater participation and lower fertility (assuming jobs are available and that they are incompatible with a woman's productive role). Women's labour characteristics indicated not only that the participation rates have increased, but that there has been a movement, from the older to the younger cohort, toward more skilled occupations in the urban areas and away from family agricultural activities in the rural areas. These productive activities are more incompatible with the reproductive role of women. In fact, in urban and rural areas, female work affected fertility when it interfered with childbearing: urban and rural work experience in services decreased the probability of occurrence of the demographic events, whereas housework and home industry did not. Occupational status at the moment of occurrence of fertility events did not show significant effects on the likelihood of occurrence of those events, suggesting that fertility decision-making is a cumulative process over life not affected by the kind of productive activity engaged in once the decision has been made.

The relationship between female work and fertility is not unidirectional but simultaneous. As female work affects fertility transitions, work transitions in turn are affected by fertility and nuptiality. Marital status and children ever born have a significant effect on the women's likelihood of entering into the labour force. Married women are more likely to work, but the presence of children affects negatively their probability of working.

Urban or rural origin among urban women did not have an important effect on the occurrence of the demographic events characterizing the family formation process. However, urban or rural place of residence plays an important role in nuptiality and fertility transitions over the life-course. Urbanites generally have access to better education, a wider spectrum of work opportunities, a better public health environment, higher access to birth-control devices and more avenues for social mobility, and they face higher costs in raising children.

Although there has been a decline in both urban and rural fertility, the levels of the rural younger cohort are as high as the levels of the urban older cohort in the upper stratum: 3.3 children. Thus, rural women's reproductive behaviour after the demographic transition is very similar to the behaviour of urban women in the best socio-economic conditions before the demographic transition. This observed behaviour concurs with the way in which women perceive the world in which they act and live. The qualification of the inherent changes of the demographic transition in the urban area indicates that there are important differences between strata in women's perceptions of circumstances influencing family formation, such as sexuality, maternity, family planning, power relationships, and female work. Urban women in the upper stratum seem to be redefining the perception and organization of their lives with a conceptual structure more attuned to the changes in their social environment. In the rural area, on the contrary, where the demographic transition started later, there are no clear differences by stratum in women's attitudes and perceptions. However, it seems that women in the upper stratum have started questioning the traditional vision of their social roles. For both urban and rural women, maternity and the role children play in their lives determine the way in which they define their lives. As a consequence, women who are now participating in productive activities have systematically assumed responsibilities outside the household without discussing the division of labour within the household. It is to be expected that in the future changes in women's perceptions of their lives will be reflected in a true reorganization and redistribution of domestic work.

Policy Implications for Colombia

The structural changes brought by development and modernization over the last three decades have had substantial effects on mortality and fertility. The government's policy towards the introduction of improvements in education and health in urban and rural areas, as well as tacit support for the private supply of birth-control devices, also has had ramifications that have contributed, through many different channels, to lower fertility and mortality rates and to accelerate the demographic transition process.

Focusing on life-histories has significant implications for political decisions, since a comparison of the experiences and characteristics of different cohorts can generate evidence to predict the characteristics and behaviour of the women who are currently in the younger cohorts. Thus, comparing our urban and rural cohorts, each one faced with different contexts, we can predict in a general way the behaviour of younger cohorts faced with changes resulting from political actions.

Urban and rural results show that management of education policies constitutes a principal instrument of intervention in the behaviour of the demographic variables of family formation and expansion. That educational levels depress fertility only above completed elementary school implies that a policy designed to increase the post-elementary schooling of all educationally disadvantaged women will have an impact on nuptiality and fertility. Additionally, every increase in the coverage of the educational system at secondary and higher levels will have a double effect on the mentioned demographic variables: a direct effect on the probability of the occurrence of the demographic events, and an indirect effect through its effect on female labour-force participation. Increases in educational attainment raise the opportunity cost of women's time and lead to higher levels of participation in productive activities, especially in the modern and/or paid activities which are incompatible with reproductive roles and affect fertility and nuptiality negatively.

Employment policies attempting to promote changes in family formation and expansion should take into account not only the influence on demographic events, but also changes in the female labour market. In particular, we have seen that higher levels of education imply not only higher participation in the labour force but at the same time a qualitative change in the labour market itself. Higher qualifications lead to non-traditional occupations, which suggest more incompatibility with reproductive roles. This shows the need to open greater opportunities for female employment in non-traditional occupations.

Employment aside, improvements in the welfare of women are particularly likely to contribute to fertility decline. As education improves a woman's social and economic opportunities, she becomes more sensitive to the costs of bearing and rearing children. Women's higher status in the home also has been shown to lower fertility among young urban women in the upper stratum.

Implications for Research and Training

The urban and rural studies described have shown that a life-course perspective on women's behaviour, as well as a time-allocation approach to household members, provides a useful approach to the understanding of micro-economic changes (at individual or household level) resulting from macro-economic changes. This study contributes both to newer methodological approaches to the problem, and furnishes a better understanding of the myriad ways families adapt to changing environmental conditions. Women's behaviour over the life-span provided a basis for research on their demographic statuses, transitions between those statuses, the co-ordination of those transitions, and the socio-economic correlates of those demographic statuses. Thus, the urban and rural studies provide insights which could be very promising for further studies in the same field.

The collection of retrospective data for generating the complete urban and rural women's event-histories provided usable, high-quality data. Thus, retrospective event-history data and the use of a life-history matrix in the collection of retrospective data is highly encouraging.

In the analysis of event-history data, urban and rural studies have shown that the use of proportional hazards models provides a powerful analytical tool that avoids several biases introduced in models based on comparisons of censored populations. Thus, the use of these models is indicated in future life-course research. Finally, since the use of statistical models for life-history data analysis is a relatively recent development, especially in developing countries, motivating their use is highly desirable. Of course, this presupposes the availability of trained researchers able to apply them. It may be necessary to start by first encouraging the use of the life-course approach in developing-country research, and by providing the necessary training for this.

APPENDIX. PROPORTIONAL HAZARDS MODELS SIMPLIFICATION

This section presents the process of model simplification for obtaining the grouped proportional hazards models of occurrence of demographic events characterizing the family formation process (first marriage and the first three parity progression ratio).

Hazard Models of the Risk of First Marriage

Tables A and B summarize the process of model simplification for the risk of marrying for the urban and rural area respectively. In these tables, the general model in both urban and rural areas refers to the estimation of separate models for each socio-economic stratum and cohort; that is, for each area we allow the baseline function *and* the set of coefficients to differ for all combinations of socio-economic stratum and cohort. The hazard function at time (or age) t for an individual in the sth socio-economic stratum and the cth cohort is defined as:

$$h_{sc}(t;Z) = h_{0sc}(t) \exp(B's_c Z)$$

where Z is the vector of covariates.

The first simplifying step was to collapse socio-economic strata within each cohort and each area. A "stratified" model was estimated where *only* socio-economic stratum was allowed to define the groups with arbitrary and unrelated baseline survivor (or hazard) functions. Thus, in this stratified model, the baseline function is allowed to differ for each socio-economic stratum and cohort, and the set of coefficients B are constrained to be identical across socio-economic strata, but allowed to vary across cohort. Thus, the hazard function for an individual in the sth socio-economic stratum and c^{th} cohort is defined as:

$$h_{sc}(t;Z) = h_{0sc}(t) \exp(B'_c Z)$$

Table A. Proportional hazards models simplification of the risk of first marriage by age, urban area

Group				General model		Grouped by stratum		Grouped by stratum and cohort	
Cohort	Stratum	N	% censor	−2 × LL	d.f.	−2 × LL	d.f.	−2 × LL	d.f.
Younger	Lower	259	12.0	2214.68	11				
	Middle	187	26.2	1251.11	11				
	Upper	132	49.2	598.75	10				
	Total	578				4078.38	11		
						(22.42	21)[a]		
						(61.57	2)[b]		
						(69.07	2)[c]		
Older	Lower	163	3.1	1324.73	11				
	Middle	187	7.0	1546.59	11				
	Upper	146	17.1	1004.16	10				
	Total	496				3905.27	11		
						(29.78	21)[a]		
						(10.99	2)[b]		
						(16.87	2)[c]		
Total		1,074						8011.08	11
								(18.42	11)[a]
								(74.38	5)[b]
								(91.42	5)[c]

a. Chi-square from the log-likelihood-ratio test.
b. Chi-square from the Generalized Wilcoxon test.
c. Chi-square from the Savage test.

Table B. Proportional hazards models simplification of the risk of first marriage by age, rural area

| Group | | N | % censor | General model | | Grouped by stratum | | Grouped by stratum and cohort | |
Cohort	Stratum			$-2 \times LL$	d.f.	$-2 \times LL$	d.f.	$-2 \times LL$	d.f.
Younger	Lower	144	21.5	984.55	12				
	Middle	181	17.1	1353.13	12				
	Upper	208	13.9	1670.85	12				
	Total	533				4031.61	12		
						(23.07	24)[a]		
						(1.55	2)[b]		
						(1.03	2)[c]		
Older	Lower	182	3.7	1416.93	11				
	Middle	201	7.5	1679.71	11				
	Upper	195	9.2	1592.26	11				
	Total	578				4715.62	11		
						(26.91	22)[a]		
						(8.44	2)[b]		
						(8.75	2)[c]		
Total		1,111						8758.69	12
								(11.26	11)[a]
								(12.29	5)[b]
								(8.14	5)[c]

a. Chi-square from the log-likelihood-ratio test.
b. Chi-square from the Generalized Wilcoxon test.
c. Chi-square from the Savage test.

The new coefficient estimates were in the range that one would expect from the coefficients in the general model. There was, however, a notable change in the new coefficient estimates, since some of them increased their statistical significance, undoubtedly a consequence of the greater statistical power obtained by combining socio-economic strata. Subsequently, it became necessary to test whether the simplification obtained by combining socio-economic strata was statistically justified. As mentioned above, in these stratified models, the various groups share the same set of b coefficients, but each stratum s has a different (unspecified) baseline survivor function. A likelihood-ratio chi-square test was used to test for the null hypothesis that the explanatory variables have identical coefficients across socio-economic strata, but different baseline survivor functions for each stratum.[1] Tables A and B also present the (-2)log-likelihood obtained in each of the general models, as well as in the model grouped by socio-economic strata for each cohort. The null hypothesis produces chi-square distributions with values that are far below the critical value for the .001 significance level, and even further below the critical value for the .10 significance level. These tests led us to conclude that the model grouped by socio-economic strata is an acceptable simplification of the general model in both urban and rural areas, and for both cohorts.

The next step in the process of simplification by socio-economic strata involved testing the null hypothesis of equality of the survivor functions between the defined groups. Generalized Wilcoxon and Savage (log-rank) tests were applied[2] and the resultant chi-square distributions are reported in tables A and B for each cohort in urban and rural areas respectively. Both tests indicated that the baseline survivor functions are statistically different between socio-economic strata, in both urban cohorts at a .01 significance level, and even at the conservative level of .001 for the younger urban cohort.

The case is not the same for the rural area. As table B indicates, these chi-square statistics from both the Wilcoxon and Savage tests for the younger cohort imply that the baseline survival functions by strata are not statistically different, whereas for the older cohort the null hypothesis of equal functions can be accepted at the .01 level, but rejected at the .05 significance level.

If we accept the null hypothesis of equal survivor functions for the defined group s for both rural cohorts, the next logical step is to check the possibility of incorporating socio-economic strata as a covariate in the models by cohort. With that aim, the corresponding rural survivor function estimates were obtained and log$[-$log $S_{0s}(t)]$ was plotted against time for each socio-economic stratum s. The resulting plots did not show constant differences over time. Because they cross, incorporating socio-economic stratum as a covariate in the model violates the proportionality assumption. Hence, it is inappropriate to incorporate socio-economic strata as a covariate. We must keep the grouped model with non-significant differences between the baseline survivor functions for each defined group.

Substantively this implies that within each cohort there are no significant differences between the baseline functions from the grouped model and from a model for the total cohort with no distinctions among socio-economic strata. Under this condition, and given the possibility of accepting the null hypothesis of different baseline survivor functions between groups at the .05 level for the older rural cohort, we took the conservative decision of accepting, for both areas and both cohorts, the simplified model grouped by socio-economic strata. However, we still have four estimated models, one for each cohort in each urban and rural area. The next step was to test whether further simplification was possible through collapsing by cohort within each area.

Results from the stratified models by socio-economic strata for each cohort once more presented a similar pattern of coefficients, and slight differences in level within each area. A new grouped model was then estimated, where the combinations of socio-economic stratum *and* cohort were used to define the groups. Thus, in this new grouped scheme, the baseline functions are allowed to be different for each (s, c) grouping, but the set of coefficients are restricted to be the same across socio-economic strata *and* across cohort. The hazard function for an individual in the sc^{th} group is defined as:

$$h_{sc}(t;Z) = h_{0sc}(t) \exp(B'Z)$$

Likelihood-ratio chi-square tests were then applied to test the null hypothesis that the explanatory variable coefficients were the same across the new defined groups (combinations of socio-economic stratum and cohort).

Tables A and B also show the log-likelihood (multiplied by -2) for the new typology by socio-economic strata and cohort within each area. Under the null hypothesis we obtain likelihood-ratio chi-square statistics far from significant in both areas, suggesting that grouping by socio-economic stratum and cohort is an acceptable simplification of the models. Since we have already rejected the hypothesis of equal baseline survivor functions for the typology based only on socio-economic strata, we expect the same results, at least for the urban area, where the test was more highly significant, when the groups are defined by both socio-economic strata and cohort. Generalized Wilcoxon and Savage tests were then applied to test this hypothesis. Tables A and B also present these results. As we expected, the chi-square statistics from both Wilcoxon and Savage tests are far from significant for the urban area. However, for rural areas the null hypothesis can be rejected for the Wilcoxon test, but accepted for the Savage test at a .05 significance level (and accepted for both tests at more conservative significance levels).

One strategy to resolve the discrepant result at the .05 level among the two tests for rural areas involves defining and utilizing a new statistic with scores intermediate to the two (Tarone and Ware, 1977). In such a case, the null hypothesis could be rejected at the .10 significant level. These results suggest that we have statistically different baseline survivor functions between the j groups defined by socio-economic stratum and cohort in both urban and rural areas. It is now acceptable to simplify by stratum and cohort. Given the steps followed, and the fact that stratum cannot be included as a covariate, we conclude that further simplification is statistically unacceptable. Starting from an extended model with 12 separate estimated models for the hazard to first marriage, our tests for simplification resulted in only two models, one for each area, both stratified by socio-economic strata and cohort.

Hazard Models of the Risk of Family Expansion Events

Proportional hazards models were estimated for the first three parity progression ratios. Similar simplification steps were followed here as in the case of the hazards models for first marriage. We first estimated the models for the hazards of having the first, the second, and the third child separately for each cohort and each socio-economic stratum for both urban and rural areas. Thus, for each parity progression, we started with 12 general models, but ended up with two models "stratified" (grouped) by socio-economic stratum and cohort.

As an example, tables C and D present the results of the process of model simplification for the risk of having the first child, for urban and rural married women, by age. Likelihood-ratio chi-square tests indicated that the simplification by socio-economic strata was statistically acceptable in both urban and rural areas (we have chi-square distributions of 26.30 with 27 degrees of freedom in the older urban cohort, and 31.96 with 28 degrees of freedom for both rural cohorts). The Savage and Wilcoxon tests also indicated that the baseline survivor functions were statistically different between socio-economic strata at a .05 significance level in both urban and rural areas. The simplification produced by collapsing cohorts can be accepted at a .001 significance level, since we obtained chi-square distributions of 25.15 and 12.56 with 14 degrees of freedom in the urban and the rural areas respectively. Generalized Wilcoxon and Savage tests are far from significant, leading to the acceptance of statistically different baseline survivor functions for each defined group (by socio-economic stratum and cohort). Thus, we ended again with acceptable simplification of the models down to two groups, one each for urban and rural area.

As a summary of the grouped models, the bottom of tables 33 to 39 (in chapter 4) presents the chi-square distributions from the generalized Wilcoxon and Savage tests, applied to test the null hypothesis of equality of the baseline survivor functions from the defined groups in each estimated model. With the exception of the rural survivor function for having the third child by age and inter-birth interval, and the rural survivor function for having the second child by inter-birth interval, all the other survival functions are statistically different between the groups at a .05 significance level.

Again, statistical differences between the groups are always larger among

Table C. Proportional hazards models simplification for the risk of first child by age, married women, urban area

| Group | | | % | General model | | Grouped by stratum | | Grouped by stratum and cohort | |
Cohort	Stratum	N	censor	−2 × LL	d.f.	−2 × LL	d.f.	−2 × LL	d.f.
Younger	Lower	213	2.3	1790.42	14				
	Middle	127	7.1	898.12	14				
	Upper	66	21.1	d					
	Total	406				3050.81	14		
						(25.40	2)b		
						(31.80	2)c		
Older	Lower	140	0.7	1038.94	14				
	Middle	162	2.0	1259.65	14				
	Upper	113	0.0	815.71	13				
	Total	415				3140.61	14		
						(26.31	27)a		
						(12.32	2)b		
						(6.91	2)c		
Total		821						6216.57	14
								(25.15	14)a
								(45.40	5)b
								(51.20	5)c

a. Chi-square from the log-likelihood-ratio test.
b. Chi-square from the Generalized Wilcoxon test.
c. Chi-square from the Savage test.
d. Too few cases for some categorical variables to converge.

Table D. Proportional hazards models simplification of the risk of first child by age, married women, rural area

Group		N	% censor	General model		Grouped by stratum		Grouped by stratum and cohort	
Cohort	Stratum			$-2 \times LL$	d.f.	$-2 \times LL$	d.f.	$-2 \times LL$	d.f.
Younger	Lower	96	2.1	670.28	14				
	Middle	128	2.3	895.74	14				
	Upper	158	3.8	1197.53	14				
	Total	382				2795.50	14		
						(31.96	28)[a]		
						(7.52	2)[b]		
						(7.55	2)[c]		
Older	Lower	139	0.0	1041.63	14				
	Middle	171	1.7	1344.54	14				
	Upper	160	2.5	1210.69	14				
	Total	470				3628.83	14		
						(31.97	28)[a]		
						(7.75	2)[b]		
						(6.40	2)[c]		
Total		852						6436.89	14
								(12.56	14)[a]
								(18.40	5)[b]
								(25.50	5)[c]

a. Chi-square from the log-likelihood-ratio test.
b. Chi-square from the Generalized Wilcoxon test.
c. Chi-square from the Savage test.

urban than among rural women, indicating more important demographic differentials and change in the former. The lack of statistical differences between the grouped rural survival functions for the second and third births indicates the absence of change in birth-spacing norms from the older to the younger rural cohorts. This is not the case for the urban area, where the generalized Wilcoxon and Savage tests indicated the highest levels of significance.

So far, data have indicated an acceptable simplification of the models grouped by socio-economic strata and cohort. The next step involves testing whether further simplification of the models is possible for the rural area showing no differences between the grouped survival functions. However, for comparison purposes between all the models at the same level of grouping, we decided to keep the rural models grouped by stratum and cohort. This decision is based on the fact that no statistical difference between the grouped survival functions suggests that the stratified models would be statistically equal to those resulting from no aggregation at all (since both the baseline survival functions and the co-efficients are not statistically different).

Proportional Hazards Models of Entering into the Labour Force

A partial likelihood procedure was used to estimate the hazards models of entering into the labour force, for each cohort and each socio-economic stratum within urban and rural areas, producing 12 estimated models. Following the methods previously mentioned, we conducted the same process of model simplification. Tables E and F present the results for urban and rural areas respectively.

The first simplification step was to collapse socio-economic strata within each cohort. A grouped model was then estimated where socio-economic stratum defined the groups. Likelihood-ratio chi-square distributions of 32.55 and 27.54 with 16 degrees of freedom were obtained for the younger and older cohorts in the urban area. For the rural area, the chi-squares obtained were 21.36 with 18 degrees of freedom and 30.75 with 17 degrees of freedom for the younger and older cohorts. Since all these values are below the critical value of the .001 significance level, we conclude that the grouped model by socio-economic stratum is an acceptable simplification of the general model in both urban and rural areas.

Chi-square distributions from the generalized Wilcoxon and Savage tests indicated that the baseline survivor functions are statistically equal in the older urban cohort, whereas they render discrepant results in the younger urban cohort. Intermediate scores supported rejection of the null hypothesis at the .01 significance level. Results of these tests for the rural area indicated equality of the survival functions in the older cohort and discrepant results in the younger cohort at a .05 significant level. The unclear evidence of statistically equal survival functions in both cohorts within each area led us to take the conservative decision of retaining the model grouped by socio-economic stratum.

Table E. Proportional hazards models simplification of the risk of first work by age, urban area

| Group | | | | General model | | Grouped by stratum | | Grouped by stratum and cohort | |
Cohort	Stratum	N	% censor	$-2 \times LL$	d.f.	$-2 \times LL$	d.f.	$-2 \times LL$	d.f.
Younger	Lower	259	24.7	1761.47	8				
	Middle	187	14.4	1379.69	8				
	Upper	132	14.4	900.54	8				
	Total	578				4074.25	8		
						(32.55	16)[a]		
						(15.99	2)[b]		
						(4.37	2)[c]		
Older	Lower	163	23.9	955.01	8				
	Middle	187	29.4	1100.67	8				
	Upper	146	24.0	858.57	8				
	Total	496				2941.79	8		
						(27.53	16)[a]		
						(1.81	2)[b]		
						(1.45	2)[c]		
Total		1,074						7040.80	8
								(24.76	8)[a]
								(43.19	5)[b]
								(62.98	5)[c]

a. Chi-square from the log-likelihood-ratio test.
b. Chi-square from the Generalized Wilcoxon test.
c. Chi-square from the Savage test.

Table F. Proportional hazards models simplification of the risk of first work by age, rural area

Cohort	Stratum	N	% censor	General model -2×LL	d.f.	Grouped by stratum -2×LL	d.f.	Grouped by stratum and cohort -2×LL	d.f.
Younger	Lower	144	59.0	408.38	9				
	Middle	181	53.6	640.49	9				
	Upper	208	38.5	1036.30	9				
	Total	533				2106.54	9		
						(21.36	18)a		
						(3.12	2)b		
						(6.06	2)c		
Older	Lower	182	65.9	465.30	8				
	Middle	201	67.7	528.60	9				
	Upper	195	51.8	811.92	9				
	Total	578				1836.58	9		
						(30.75	17)a		
						(7.61	2)b		
						(10.24	2)c		
Total		1,111						3949.26	9
								(6.14	9)a
								(55.43	5)b
								(64.39	5)c

a. Chi-square from the log-likelihood-ratio test.
b. Chi-square from the Generalized Wilcoxon test.
c. Chi-square from the Savage test.

The next step was to determine whether further simplification would be possible. A new grouped model by socio-economic stratum and cohort was then estimated for each urban and rural area. Under the null hypothesis of equal explanatory variables across groups, we obtained chi-square distributions of 24.76 with 8 degrees of freedom in the urban area and 6.14 with 9 degrees of freedom in the rural area. The last value is far from significant. The first one, for the urban area, allowed us to accept the null hypothesis at a .001 significance level, but reject it at a .01 level. Being conservative again led us to accept the simplification of the models. Generalized Wilcoxon and Savage tests gave chi-square distributions far from significant, indicating that the baseline survivor functions for each defined group are statistically different. Thus, the process of model simplification resulted in two aggregate models, one for each area, for the hazard of entering into the labour force (first job).

NOTES

Chapter 1

1. Life expectancy (at birth) is the average number of years a person can expect to live based on the mortality rates currently experienced by persons at each age.
2. The total fertility rate is the number of births that a woman would have at the end of her reproductive period, that is by age 50, if she behaved according to the current age-specific fertility pattern.
3. A birth cohort (generally called cohort) is a group of persons born in the same period of time. Thus, persons in the same age-group belong to the same birth cohort.

Chapter 2

1. The relation between the frequency of first marriages in the present cohort and the standard frequencies can be represented by the analytical expression developed by Coale and McNeil (1972):

$$g(a) = G(w)(0,1947/k)exp((-0,174/k)(a - a_0 - 6,06k) - exp(-0,2881/k)(a - a_0 - 6,06k)).$$

2. Because the mean age of the standard pattern is 11.36 when $k = 1.0$, in the adjusted pattern SMAM = a_0 + 11.36k.
3. A fertility model pattern by specific age is given by the equation:

$$f(a) = G(a) r(a) = G(a) M n exp(m v(a))$$

where: $f(a)$ is the age-specific fertility pattern; $G(a)$ is the proportion of those ever married (from the population pattern characterized by the parameters a_0, k and G(w)); $n(a)$ is the natural marital fertility pattern; and $v(a)$ is the typical pattern of deviation from natural fertility. $n(a)$ and $v(a)$ have been empirically determined (Coale and Trussell, 1974).
4. The proportionality assumption is that the relation of the risk function between two individuals with different covariates does not depend on time t (age or duration).

5. The model can also be expressed in terms of the survival function instead of the risk function.
6. For this reason, urban study and Bogotá study refer to the same study.
7. From here on, in the urban study the "older cohort" refers to the 45–49 cohort and the "younger cohort" to the 25–29 cohort.
8. This region has an altitude similar to Bogotá, between the medium and the higher thermic floors, over 1,500 metres above sea level.
9. The DRI programme is sponsored by the Department of Agriculture, which via credit programmes, infrastructure investments, and technical assistance promotes higher production by improving production conditions in field economic units.
10. The cohorts were not the same as in the urban study, 25–29 and 45–49, in order to avoid subsampling techniques which would then have to be applied. Since the size of the two cohorts was not the same because of the population's age distribution, it would have then been necessary to cover a larger rural area and randomly select women from the larger (younger) cohort to end up with the same number of women in each cohort. It was decided, instead, to increase the age-range of the smaller (older) cohort.
11. From here on, in the rural study "older cohort" refers to the 40–49 cohort and "younger cohort" refers to the 25–31 cohort.
12. It was not possible to have a pre-stratified sample because of a lack of sufficient information.
13. A factor analysis was used to determine the degree of living conditions. Two sets of variables were considered: variables related to rural characteristics, such as isolation and access to urban centres; and variables related to population living conditions, such as characteristics of the dwellings and the households (sewerage connection, tenancy relation, main source of support), the existence of and accessibility to public and community services (school, health centre, drugstore, water supply, electric power), and finally the community organization (community action board, DRI committees, co-operatives).
14. Abortion, for example, was approached from the legal point of view (crime), from the moral (sin), and from the medical point of view.

Chapter 3

1. As mentioned before, DRI stands for the government programme, Desarrollo Rural Integrado (Integrated Rural Development).
2. Waste dwellings are built with impermanent materials such as plastic, paper, card, etc.
3. Since women in the older cohorts have been exposed to migration for a longer period of time, comparisons between cohorts are not considered here.
4. In the Colombian educational system, primary school means five years of schooling, secondary school the next six years, and superior education anything above 12 years of schooling.
5. As mentioned before, family plot activities are identified as subsistence activities, while farm activities are those performed mainly for commercial purposes, although they may also include subsistence production.

6. Changes in jobs may or may not mean changes in occupation.
7. Marriage refers to legal and consensual unions.
8. This is fully explored in the next chapter when we look at the family formation process.

Chapter 4

1. See chapter 3, note 7.
2. Housework includes internal domestic service, that is, domestic servants living in the house where they work.
3. If female work activity referred to the year of occurrence of the event, we would not be able to tell whether a woman was out of the labour force because she had a child, or had a child because she was not working.
4. We have, in fact, very simple life-histories. Only a small number of statuses are observed in the considered life domains. For a complete analysis of time allocation between statuses along the life-course of this sample of women, see Florez and Hogan, (1988b).
5. As was explained in chapter 2, "stratified" models divide the data into "strata" according to the values of the considered categorical variable. Given that we have socio-economic strata, the "strata" in the models will be instead called "groups."
6. The subroutine 2L-Cox Models of the BMDP computer program was used.
7. Although the results for these models and for each one of the following estimated models are not inluded here, a complete presentation is done in the final reports for each one of the urban and rural studies (see Florez, Bonilla, and Echeverri, 1985, 1987).
8. The complete process of model simplification for each considered event with its corresponding statistical tests is presented in the Appendix.
9. Although we could test whether further simplification is possible through collapsing by area (urban and rural), it is not our purpose to do so here.
10. In fact, models for the risk of first child were estimated for both married and all women, and the coefficients for use of family planning were opposite even when we controlled for marital status in the models for all women.
11. Although some of those studies control for husband's education, the inverted-"U" pattern is still observed. In our case, only women's information is available.
12. Female labour-force participation rate at age a, p(a), and female employment rate at age a, e(a), are defined, respectively, by:

$$p(a) = \frac{E(a) + U(a)}{F(a)} \qquad e(a) = \frac{E(a)}{F(a)}$$

where: $E(a)$ is the employed female population at age a; $U(a)$ is the unemployed female population at age a; $F(a)$ is the total female population at age a.
13. A complete description of the process of simplification is presented in the Appendix.
14. Mincer (1985) also finds this pattern in developed countries and suggests that it is partly due to the definition of work (e.g. farm and self-employment are less educated and more likely to work).

Chapter 5

1. A complete analysis can be found in the urban and rural final reports (Florez, Bonilla, and Echeverri, 1985, 1987).
2. The ethnomethodological perspective is little known in Latin America. Here we recognize the valuable assistance of Dr Rod Watson, University of Manchester, in the potential utility of this perspective for the analysis of women's perceptions. The analysis presented here has benefited from these reflections, although it is not strictly an ethnomethodological exercise.
3. See for example Michel Foucault (1982), Hortz Kurnitzki (1980), and Elssy Bonilla (1986).
4. The importance of the maternity role in the woman's conceptualization has been considered by several authors: Nancy Chorodov (1984), Ann Oakley (1981), Elssy Bonilla (1985).
5. An analysis of the way in which the Colombian family is centred on male authority is found in Ferrufino (1985). In this section patriarchy is understood to be the social organization of ethical, legal, and political relations which give men authority over women and subordinate women within family structures.
6. An analysis of the intensity of female work in Colombia was made by Nohra Rey de Marulanda (1981).

Appendix

1. This test statistic is constructed by calculating twice the positive difference between the sum of the log-likelihood of each one of the expanded estimated models and the log-likelihood of the "stratified" model, with degrees of freedom defined by the number of constraints that distinguish the two models.
2. The tests differ in the way the observations are weighted. The Wilcoxon test gives greater weight to early observations and is less sensitive to late events.

REFERENCES

Abeles, R., and M. Riley. 1974. *A Life Course Perspective on the Latter Years of Life: Some Implications for Research*. Social Science Research Council, New York.

Allison, Paul D. 1984. *Event History Analysis: Regression for Longitudinal Event Data*. Sage University Paper Series on Quantitative Applications in the Social Sciences, Series Number 07-046. Sage, Beverly Hills/London/New Delhi.

Aponte de Pieschacon, C., et al. 1985. Anotaciones acerca de la violencia sobre la mujer en Bogotá. Paper presented at the International Meeting of Group Psychodrama and Psychotherapy, Buenos Aires.

Baltes, P., and Orville G. Brim, eds. 1979. *Life Span Development and Human Behavior*, vol. 2. Academic Press, New York.

Banguero, Harold, et al. 1983. *Desarrollo socioeconomico y cambio poblacional en Colombia*. Centro de Estudios sobre Desarrollo Económico, CEDE, Facultad de Economía, Universidad de Los Andes, Bogotá.

Becker, Gary. 1960. An Economic Analysis of Fertility. In: *Demographic and Economic Change in Developed Countries*. Princeton University Press, Princeton, N.J.

———. 1965. A Theory of Allocation of Time. *Economic Journal*, 75:493–517.

Berkner, L. 1975. The Use and Misuse of Census Data for the Historical Analysis of Family Structure. *Journal of Interdisciplinary History*, 4:721–738.

Bonilla, Elssy. 1985. *Mujer y familia en Colombia*. Plaza y Janes, Bogotá.

———. 1986. Poder patriarcal: Una constante social? *Texto y contexto* (Bogotá), 7:11–34.

Bonilla, E., and E. Velez. 1987. *Mujer y trabajo en el sector rural colombiano*. Plaza y Janes, Bogotá.

Breslow, N.E. 1974. Covariance Analysis of Censored Survival Data. *Biometrics*, 30:89–99.

Caldwell, John. 1982. *Theory of Fertility Decline*. Academic Press, New York.

Campillo, F., and C. Garca. 1984. *Situación social de la población rural colombiana*. Ministerio de Agricultura, Bogotá.

Chorodov, N. 1984. *The Reproduction of Mothering: Psychoanalysis and the Sociology of Gender*. University of California Press.

Coale, Ansley. 1971. Age Patterns of Marriage. *Population Studies*, 25(2):193–214.

———. 1973. The Demographic Transition Reconsidered. In: *International Population Conference*, vol. I. International Union for the Scientific Study of Population, Liège.

———. 1977. The Development of New Models of Nuptiality and Fertility. *Population* (special number), 131–154.

Coale, Ansley, and D.R. McNeil. 1972. Distribution by Age of the Frequency of First Marriage in a Female Cohort. *Journal of the American Statistical Association*, 67:743–749.

Coale, Ansley, and James Trussell. 1974. Model Fertility Schedules. *Population Index*, 40(2):1985–258.

———. 1975. Erratum. *Population Index*, 41(4):572.

———. 1978. Technical Note: Finding the Two Parameters that Specify a Model Schedule of Marital Fertility. *Population Index*, 44(2):203–211.

Cochrane, Susan. 1983. Effects of Education and Urbanization on Fertility. In: R.A. Bulatao and R.D. Lee et al., eds., *Determinants of Fertility in Developing Countries*, vol. II. Academic Press, New York.

Cox, D.R. 1972. Regression Models and Life Tables. *Journal of the Royal Statistical Society*, Series B 34, 187–202.

Cuff, E.C., and G.C.F. Payne, eds. 1985. *Perspectives in Sociology*. George Allen & Unwin, London.

Departamento Administrativo National de Estadística, DANE. 1938, 1951, 1964, 1973, 1985. *Censos colombianos de población y vivienda*.

———. 1982. Descripción del recuento de edificaciones y vivienda de Bogotá, D.E. 1980. *Boletin mensual de estadística*, 375 (October).

Elder, J. Glen. 1975. Age Differentiation and the Life Course. *Annual Review of Sociology*, 1:165–191.

———. 1978. Approaches to Social Change and the Family. *American Journal of Sociology*, 84:S1–S38.

———. 1981. History and the Family: The Discovery of Complexity. *Journal of Marriage and the Family*, 43:489–519.

Espenshade, T., and Rachel E. Braun. 1982. Life Course Analysis and Multistage Demography: An Application to Marriage, Divorce and Remarriage. *Journal of Marriage and the Family*, 44(4):1025–1036.

Featherman, David. 1980. Retrospective Longitudinal Research: Methodological Considerations. *Journal of Economics and Business*, 32:152–169.

———. 1983. The Life-span Perspectives in Social Science Research. In: Paul B. Baltes and Orville G. Brim, Jr., eds., *Life Span Development and Human Behaviour*. Vol. 5, pp. 1–57. Academic Press, New York.

Ferrufino, L. 1985. *Antropología y familia*. Tercer Mundo, Bogotá.

Florez, C. Elisa, Elssy Bonilla, and Rafael Echeverri, 1985. *The Impact of the Demographic Transition on Households in Bogotá*. CEDE Reports. Centro de Estudios sobre Desarrollo Económico (CEDE), Facultad de Economía, Universidad de Los Andes, Bogotá.

———. 1987. *The Meaning of the Demographic Transition on Households of a Colombian Rural Setting*. CEDE Reports. Centro de Estudios sobre Desarrollo Económico (CEDE), Facultad de Economía, Universidad de los Andes, Bogotá.

Florez, C. Elisa, Rafael Echeverri, and Regina Mendez. 1987. *Análisis demográfico del censo de 1985: Fecundidad*. CEDE Reports. Centro de Estudios sobre Desarrollo Económico (CEDE), Facultad de Economía, Universidad de Los Andes, Bogotá.

Florez, C. Elisa, and Dennis Hogan. 1988a. Women's Status and Infant Mortality in Rural Colombia. Under review at *Social Biology*.

——. 1988b. Demographic Transition and Life-course Change in Colombia. Under review at *Journal of Family History*.

Foner, Anne, and David Ketzer. 1978. Transitions over the Life Course: Lessons from Age-set Societies. *American Journal of Sociology*, 83:1081–1104.

Foucault, M. 1982. *La historia de la sexualidad*. Siglo XXI, Mexico City.

Freedman, Ronald. 1979. Theories of Fertility Decline: A Reappraisal. *Social Forces*, 58:1–17.

Gomez, Elsa. 1981. *La formación de la familia y la participación laboral en Colombia*. CELADE, series D, no. 104. CELADE, Santiago de Chile.

Hajnal, J. 1965. Age at Marriage and Proportions Marring. *Population Studies*, 7:111–136.

Henry, Louis. 1961. Some Data on Natural Fertility. *Eugenics Quarterly*, 8(2):81–91.

Hogan, Dennis. 1981. *Transition and Social Change: The Early Lives of American Men*. Academic Press, New York.

——. 1985. The Demography of Life-span Transitions: Temporal and Gender Comparisons. In: Alice Rossi, ed., *Gender and the Life Course*. Aldine, New York.

Holford, T.R. 1976. Life Tables with Concomitant Information. *Biometrics*, 32:587–598.

Kalbfleisch, John, and Ross Prentice. 1980. *The Statistical Analysis of Failure Time Data*. Wiley & Sons, New York.

Karweit, Nancy. 1987. *CASA: A Data Base Management System for Event Histories*. Johns Hopkins University, Baltimore.

Kertzer, David, and Andrea Schiaffino. 1983a. Industrialization and Coresidence: A Life Course Approach. In: P. Baltes and Orville G. Brim, eds., *Life Span Development and Human Behavior*. Vol. 5, pp. 360–391. Academic Press, New York.

——. 1983b. *New Perspectives on Old Households: Toward a Processual of Coresidence*. National Institute of Child Health and Human Development.

——. 1983c. Historical Demographic Methods of Life Course Study. In: *New Methods of Old Age Research*, 2nd. ed.

Knodel, John. 1977. Family Limitation and the Fertility Transition: Evidence from the Age Patterns of Fertility in Europe and Asia. *Population Studies*, 31:219–249.

Kurnitzki, Hortz. 1980. *El origen libidinal del dinero*. Siglo XXI, Mexico City.

Liker, R. 1932. A New Technique for the Measurement of Attitudes. *Archives of Psychology*, 140:1–55.

Lopez, C., and M. Leal. 1977. El trabajo de la mujer. In: M. Leon, ed., *La mujer y el desarrollo en Colombia*. ACEP, Bogotá.

Mason, O. Karen. 1983. *The Status of Women, Fertility and Mortality: A Review of Interrelationships*. Population Studies Division, Rockefeller Foundation, New York.

Mauldin, P., and B. Berelson. 1978. Conditions of Fertility Decline in Developing Countries 1965–1975. *Studies in Family Planning*, 9(5).

Menken, J., J. Trussell, D. Stempel, and O. Babakol. 1981. Proportional Hazards Life Table Models: An Illustrative Analysis of Socio-demographic Influences on Marriage Dissolution in the United States. *Demography*, 18:181–200.

Minage-Klenova, W. 1980. Does Labor Time Decrease with Industrialization? A Survey of Time Allocation Studies. *Current Anthropology*, 21(3).

Mincer, J. 1985. Trends in Women's Work, Education and Family Building. *Journal of Labor Economics*, 3, 1(2):753–3347.

Munroe, R., et al, eds. 1981. *Handbook of Cross-cultural Human Development*. STPM Press, New York.

Namboodiri, K., and C.M. Suchindran. 1987. *Life Table Techniques and their Applications*. Academic Press, New York.

Oakley, A. 1981. *From Here to Maternity: Becoming a Mother*. Penguin Books, Harmondsworth.

———. 1979. Prevalencia del uso de anticoncepción en Colombia: Determinantes e implicaciones. *Estudios de población* (Bogotá), 5(7).

Ochoa, Luis Hernando. 1982. El descenso de la fecundidad en Colombia y sus implicaciones demográficas. In: Luis Hernando Ochoa, ed., *Implicaciones demográficas del descenso de la fecundidad en Colombia*. Mongrafía de la Corporación Centro Regional de Población (CCRP), vol. 18. CCRP, Bogotá.

Patton. 1980. *Qualitative Evaluation Models*. Sage, Beverly Hills, Calif.

Potter, J., M. Ordonez, and A.R. Meashman. 1976. The Rapid Decline in Colombian Fertility. *Population and Development Review*, 2:509–528.

Rey de Marulanda, Nohra. 1981. *El trabajo de la mujer*. Documentos del Centro de Estudios sobre Desarrollo Económico (CEDE), no. 063. Facultad de Economía, Universidad de Los Andes, Bogotá.

Rey de Marulanda, N., and U. Ayala. 1979. La reproducción de la fuerza de trabajo en las grandes ciudades colombianas. *Desarrollo y sociedad*, 1:11–36.

Riley, Matilda. 1973. Aging and Cohort Succession: Interpretations and Misinterpretations. *Public Opinion Quarterly*, 37:35–49.

———. 1985. Age Strata in Social Systems. In: R.H. Binstock and E. Shanas, ed., *Handbook of Aging and the Social Sciences*, 2nd. ed. Van Nostrand Reinhold, New York.

Rodriguez, German, and John Hobcraft. 1980. *Illustrative Analysis: Life Tables Analysis of Birth Intervals in Colombia*. WFS Scientific Reports, no. 16. WFS, London.

Ryder, Norman. 1965. The Cohort as a Concept in the Study of Social Change. *American Sociological Review*, 30:843–861.

Sanz de Santamaría, M.C. 1986. Aborto y mujer en Bogotá. In: Elssy Bonilla, ed., *Mujer y sociedad en los paises del Tercer Mundo*. In press.

Sise–Departamento Administrativo Nacional de Estadística (DANE). 1982. Recuento de edificaciones y vivienda de Bogotá. *Boletín mensual de estadística* (Bogotá), 375.

Sorensen, Aage. 1980. Analysis of Change in Discrete Variables. In: J. Clubb and E. Schuech, eds., *Historical Social Research*. Klett-Cotta, Stuttgart.

Spradley, J.R. 1986. *Participant Observation*. Holt, Rinehart & Winston, New York.

Standing, G. 1978. *Labour Force Participation and Development*. International Labour Organization, Geneva.

Tarone, R., and J. Ware. 1977. On Distributions-free tests for Equality of Survival Distributions. *Biometrika*, 64:156–160.

Teachman, Jay. 1982. Methodological Issues in the Analysis of Family Formation and Dissolution. *Journal of Marriage and the Family*, 44(4):1037.

Thomas, F. 1985. *Los universos masculinos y femeninos en algunos discursos en los medios masivos en Colombia*. Departamento de Psicología, Universidad Nacional, Bogotá.

Trussell, James, and Charles Hammerslough. 1983. A Hazards Model Analysis of the Covariates of Infant and Child Mortality in Sri Lanka. *Demography*, 20:1–26.

Tuma, Nancy, and Michael Hannan. 1984. *Social Dynamics: Models and Methods*. Academic Press, New York.

Tuma, Nancy, Michael Hannan, and Lyle Groeneveld. 1979. Dynamic Analysis of Event Histories. *American Journal of Sociology*, 84:820–854.

United Nations. 1984. Compiling Social Indicators on the Situation of Women. UN Studies in Methods, series F, no. 32. United Nations, New York.

————. 1985. *Women's Employment and Fertility: A Comparative Analysis of World Fertility Survey Results for 38 Developing Countries.* United Nations, New York.

Watson, R. 1986. Algunas recomendaciones sobre la aplicabilidad del metodo etnológico para el estudio de la transición rural del UNU. Mimeo.

Willis, Robert. 1973. A New Approach to the Economic Theory of Fertility Behavior. *Journal of Political Economy*, 81:S14–S64.